Tell It Sister, Tell It

★

ISBN: 0615443141
EAN-13: 9780615443140

Tell It Sister, Tell It

MEMORIES, MUSIC AND MIRACLES

Stella Parton

Preface

I will never be able to thank all those who have helped me along the way. So many little angels have touched my life or the life of someone in my family. First, I thank God for giving me life and wonderful health. I thank my parents, Robert Lee Parton and Avie Lee Owens Parton, for bringing me into this world and loving me. I thank my grandparents on both sides and my aunts and uncles, too many to mention by name, my brothers and sisters, nieces and nephews — basically the whole big clan, Darlene Tatum for helping me with my son, Tim for nine years, and Brenda Madden for all her hard work and loyalty over the last several years. Gerry Wood for his help in transcribing my first batch of tapes, Brant Moll and Bill Reid for their continued encouragement and loyalty. Joe Taylor for all the shows he booked over the years — Joe, I couldn't have done it without you. Timothy Rauhoff, for being such a wonderful son; for having the love, respect and patience to read, correct and improve what is written here and to all of you, you know who you are, for your loyalty, love, support and inspiration. To those of you who haven't wished me well, you've propelled me onward. I forgive you and God loves you just as He loves me.

The idea for this book came about because of changes taking place in my life and the lives of those around me. While driving down the highway one afternoon it hit me like a bolt out of the blue—Stella, why not write an inspirational book about your own life? I've been asked to write a book many times throughout the years.

I realize through the writing of this book that there is always more than one way to look at things. We all have a different take.

The challenge has been to write about my family and my experiences growing up. I love my family very much. The lessons and experiences with them shaped my life. I'm grateful for the goodness of my parents and grandparents.

I am thankful to have grown up with so many siblings and cousins. Being from such a large family taught me early on to be unselfish and to look out for the care of others. Birth order has a lot to do with how we behave in a family.

Going through the process of reflecting on my life through these pages, I have come to realize no one is perfect. I am just like everyone else; doing the best I can with the information I have to work with. I have discovered a lot about what has shaped me as a human being and as a woman.

I have been darn lucky in some ways and not so lucky in others. I am glad to be an American. I am thankful I was taught the importance of a spiritual life very early; it has sustained me through times of struggle.

I will never get it all figured out but who does? I believe we truly are just passing through this life. The older I get the more I understand—"you can't take it with you." So leave as much goodness as you can, for that is all that will remain.

I decided to write this book with the hope of healing not only some of my own wounds, but to help others. We are never alone. Each day we cope with issues. I believe we need courage, boldness and a double portion of love to enjoy our lives. I hope you have some laughter along the way as well.

I'm pretty good at a few things. One in particular is being loyal to my family and friends. Mom would always say that I was like the mouse in the quilt scraps because I kept to myself as much as possible and tried to do as I was told. She said that's how I always avoided getting into trouble when the older kids had to be punished for talking back or not doing what they were told. It didn't take a genius to figure out how to avoid getting the belt from Daddy when he came home from work. On the other hand, Daddy used to say about me, "Don't get Stel mad, 'cause she has the temper of a wildcat, but she is the one with the tender heart." All my siblings have good hearts, but he just said that to excuse my temper, I guess.

I have always tried to treat everyone, as I want to be treated. I naturally assume everyone else is the same until they prove otherwise. I've been told I'm too trusting. Needless to say, Mama and Daddy could always get me to admit to the truth because of my "guilty little conscience," as one of my siblings always says. It wasn't always the most popular way to be, mind you. Dolly always says, "Don't ask Stella what she thinks unless you want to hear the truth." They've all learned that about me and don't ask my opinion much anymore.

Don't get me wrong here. I am no goody two-shoes. I have many faults, but that's another book to write, when I'm older and the rest of my siblings are so old they can't read. I've heard it said that, "God takes care of fools and children." It's obvious I'm not a kid anymore. Oh well.

I wish I had all the answers or a secret formula to life but the *truth* is the secret to *my* life. I tell the truth as much as I know it. First, for myself and then for those that it concerns.

I say nothing at all if the truth can't be acknowledged. After all, the Bible says to know the truth will set you free.

Isn't that what we all seek—freedom for our spirits so that we can grow onward? I have the sneaky suspicion that the older we get the closer we get to our own truth. By the time we get to the end, we suddenly realize we knew what it was all along. It's all about self-acceptance, loving everyone, and forgiving everyone. When we can do that, then we experience the true miracle of life. Sounds like heaven to me.

This book is dedicated to the memory of all the women and children who have lost their lives from domestic violence abuse. You are not forgotten.

A portion of the proceeds from this book will go to domestic violence shelters.

Disclaimer:

To all my siblings, relatives and friends—I may have a date, amount or whatever wrong, but it's my story and I'm sticking to it, so just get over it. I'm just sayin'.

Love you always and forever,
Stella.

Foreword

She's a miracle worker, an answer to a prayer, a passionate and sensitive woman, a real beauty and a real hoot. She writes from experience and from the soul; from hurt, and from the heart; from love and from love gone wrong.

She is special, she's my friend. She's Stella Parton. Or "Stella." as she's calling herself these days for an important reason explained in this book. She's a foul-weather friend, always there to hold your hand tightly through the dark valleys and lift it high on the glorious mountaintops where her footsteps lead.

Need I say more about Stella.? No. But I will anyway. Her laughter tinkles like wind chimes in a soft Smoky Mountain breeze. Her eyes sparkle with the heady mix of mountain insight and user-friendly frivolity. Her smile warms, her touch heals, and her spirit soars. She makes me laugh, she makes me cry—sometimes simultaneously.

I admire her for so many reasons. She shattered glass ceilings in Nashville with the same self-assured wisdom and confidence that had crumbled the confining coal ceilings of her Appalachian mountains. She flashes the courage to follow her impressive talents into the realms of songwriting, singing and acting despite looming in the shadow of a sister superstar also named Parton who has conquered those same three professions. Stella. knows the gain and pain of a last name. Trust me, there's more of the latter than the former. But she has shattered the surname ceiling, an angel flying too close to the ground, her own woman, following her own muse, hearing her own unique drummer. A crown princess who delights in leading the entourage off the beaten path into places dark, delightful and demanding. Stella. successfully stepped out of the shadow that would have snuffed out lesser lights and strode boldly into the deceptive glamour and unforgiving glare of stage lights. She swapped shadows for sunlight, and the world is a brighter and better place because of it.

Stella. has become my earth angel. Her name imprints this book with passion, patience and perseverance—credentials and qualities any angel dealing with me would find as essentials in their job descriptions. In these pages, I hope Stella. becomes your angel, too. God couldn't give you a better one.

– Gerry Wood, Nashville, 2010

Miracle - 1: an extraordinary event manifesting divine in-tervention in human affairs ***2:*** an extremely outstanding or unusual event, thing, or accomplishment

—Webster's New Collegiate Dictionary

Tell It Sister Tell It

Tell it sister tell it everywhere you go
Tell it sister tell it let everybody know
Sing all through the night
Make us feel all right
Tell it sister tell it everywhere you go

"Tell It Sister Tell It"
Written by: Stella Parton
© 2003 My Mama's Music (BMI)

Table of Contents

music

miracles

memories

*My first grade picture. Willadeene bought me the pretty green dress
with red buttons on the collar with her babysitting money.*
(Courtesy of the Attic Entertainment Archives)

My beautiful Mama. She always said she was prettier
than all of her daughters. She was right.
(Courtesy of the Attic Entertainment Archives)

Getting a hug from Daddy.
(Courtesy of the Attic Entertainment Archives)

Aunt Dorothy Jo, her daughter, Rena and Me at the Ryman Auditorium.
(Courtesy of the Attic Entertainment Archives)

Back row (left to right): Cassie, cousin Donna Faye, Me, David;
Front row (left to right): Bobby, Denver, Dolly, Willadeene and Randy.
(Photo by Estelle Watson. Courtesy of the Family Archives.)

Owens-Parton family gathering. Front row (left to right): Cassie, Uncle Lester, cousin Donna Faye. Second row (left to right): Me, cousin Dale, Denver, Bobby and Dolly. Third row (left to right): Grandma Rena, Grandpa Jake, Aunt Estelle, David, Willadeene, Aunt Dorothy Jo and Mama.
(Photo by Estelle Watson. Courtesy of the Family Archives.)

I'm sure I was thinking that's enough pictures for one day. Back row (left to right): Willadeene, David, and Randy. Center row (left to right): Dolly and Denver. Front row (left to right): Bobby, Me and Cassie.
(Photo by Lily Owens Huskey—Courtesy of the Family Archives)

My precious Dad and Mom.
(Courtesy of the Family Archives.)

Mama and Daddy on their way to a concert at Dollywood.
(Courtesy of the Family Archives.)

*"If we forget our past, we won't remember our future,
because we won't have one."*

– Flannery O'Conner

He's God's Baby Now

O verpowered by the smell of funeral flowers and perfume, I could hardly breathe. It's a miracle how God
allows us to go on autopilot or into "shock" at a time
like this. Perhaps it's so we can tolerate the pain.

There he lay in that beautiful mahogany casket, his head
on a fluffy white pillow. Somehow, he seemed so small. My
handsome Daddy with the long curly eyelashes, now closed
were those beautiful blue eyes. I could see why the women
had all liked him so much with those blonde curls, sweet
smile and more charm than Billy Graham and Kirk Douglas
rolled into one. He just had a way about him. I can also understand why Mama loved him more than all of her children.

My sister Cassie insisted we stand in a receiving line according to birth order to receive family and friends at the
funeral home. Instead, I decided I would stand near Daddy
at the head of his casket. I wanted to be close to him for as
long as possible. How could he look so small when he had
always been as big as God to me while I was growing up?

Daddy worked hard and drank hard except for the last seven years of his life. He had gotten saved, or should I say, "repented." When I was five, I recall that Daddy had "lived right" for a while until some of the church folks did some things that hurt him deeply. It shook his faith and he backslid.

Daddy always loved his family and was always proud of his "young'uns" as we say in the mountains. He always made sure we had food on the table and a roof over our heads. As he would say, "Don't mess with my young 'uns." He would have killed anybody who hurt one of us.

Mama and Daddy had a deep love affair that lasted almost sixty years, but they had their problems. They split a couple of times, once when Mama was pregnant with my oldest sister, Willadeene, and once for several years while they were in their late fifties. Both times, Daddy fathered children by other women, but somehow he would always come back home to Mama when she decided to forgive him. She had given him twelve children and would have kept on going if the doctors hadn't cut her "baby bag" out after Rachel was born. That's what my Mama called her uterus. I don't think she ever forgave the doctor for stopping her breeding.

The funeral home was crowded that night, and all sorts of people—friends and relatives none of us had seen in years and some we had never seen—were coming through the line. Why, one woman even had the nerve to ask Dolly for an autograph. I was nauseated by her insensitivity.

Suddenly I looked up from stroking Daddy's soft silver locks, the hair that I had stroked since I was a little girl. There she stood, my half-sister, Laura, with tears streaming down her face. It was like looking into my own face or that of one of my other full siblings. In a soft trembling voice, she asked, "You're Stella, aren't you?" I said, "Yes, and you must be Laura.

I am so glad you are here. Daddy would be glad you came as well. Let me introduce you to the rest of us." It took a lot of courage at her young age to walk up to that many brothers and sisters she had never met. I think she must have been around eighteen. And as we say in the mountains, she's a Parton all right.

A few years earlier, one of her half-brothers had brought me a picture of her, and I sent her some makeup in a caboodle box with a note. One Sunday evening, I took the picture over to Daddy and watched him stare at it. He held it tenderly just as he had held all of his children and grandchildren as they were born. Daddy felt bad on some levels about the choices he had made, as we all do, but he had a very loving heart. His home, family, country, and community were what he cared about most.

With my half-brother, Glenn, and my half-sister, Laura, in the line with the rest of us, I felt Daddy had come full circle somehow having all of his children together for the first time. Glenn was born between Denver and Dolly during one of Daddy and Mama's separations. I had only met Glenn one time before; however, he looked more like Daddy than all of my brothers, which stung a little. This was a surreal moment for all of us. I took Laura by the hand and walked around the room introducing her to all the siblings and the grandchildren. I suddenly became aware of God's unconditional love for us. Even in our pain and great loss, God had given us Laura and Glenn and He gave us to them as well.

My brother, Randy, walked over to the casket beside me and as he lovingly looked down at Daddy, he softly whispered in my ear, "Stel, he's God's baby now," and at that moment, I understood that's exactly it. We are all God's babies. We just need to realize it. I saw the miracle in it.

Ever since that moment, I look at everyone as God's babies. No matter what the circumstances may be, we need to try as best we can to love on that level. So often, I have seen people act as if they have a "corner on the market" in Heaven when just a little more love and kindness could make a world of difference in the life of someone who feels unworthy of God's love and mercy.

"No man can know where he's going unless
he knows exactly where he's been."

– *Maya Angelou*

My Appalachian Home

I am the kind of person I am because of growing up so close to nature. The purity and richness that grace the Appalachian Mountains offer a comforting feeling like no other place on earth.

When I was very young, we lived in a small wood frame house that consisted of four small rooms: a living room, kitchen and two tiny bedrooms. The floors were wood with linoleum rugs covering them and sometimes no rugs at all. We had a wood-burning stove in the kitchen. We cooled our butter and milk in the spring out behind the house. We had coal oil lamps to light our house in the evenings. There was no electricity, telephone or even a radio in my first memories of home. In the summer time, we spent most of our time outside. We had a covered porch on the front and the back. There were cane bottomed, straight backed chairs on the front porch where we spent many hours. My mother read the Bible to us quite often there when we were young. Those Bible stories were wonderful; they still live in my mind today and I cherish those memories. I can still hear her voice mixed in with the sound of the birds and the crickets as they flew by.

Mama, Daddy, and visiting relatives would congregate there on the porch and tell stories as they watched us kids play in the yard. We had a small stream that ran by in front of the house. It had been dammed up with rocks for Mama to collect water to do our washing on a scrub board. She heated water in large, black cast iron kettles and I can still smell the wood burning as she stoked the fire underneath the kettles on laundry day. These same kettles were used to make lard and cracklings from the butchering of the hogs in the fall. Mama also made lye soap from the same scraps that were left over from the "hog killing" as it was called. The lye soap was used as detergent for the clothes and for other household cleaning chores. You cannot have a bad complexion if you use this type of soap. We also bathed with it.

When the swimming hole was not being used for household chores, we children played in it. Once when I was four or five, I lost my footing and fell under the water. All I remember is the sun in my face as my big brother, David was leaning over me pushing the water out of my lungs. Needless to say, I was a bit afraid of water after that and never really learned to swim.

We lived on a strict budget, but sometimes if we had earned a quarter from setting tobacco or picking blackberries for some of the neighbors, we bought a Coke and a candy bar. Candy bars were bigger then and only cost a nickel. Of course, we knew which ones were the biggest and usually bought the Three Musketeers bar or the Zero bar.

My parents were proud and very self-reliant. I'm sure they learned this behavior from growing up so hard in the mountains during the depression. I've heard it said…"We didn't even know there was a 'great depression.'" I guess things never changed that much in the mountains.

However, stubborn pride and independence are beautiful qualities displayed by the Appalachian people, and it's helped to create a very unique culture.

We accept a hand *up*, but only if we are treated with dignity. We refuse to take a hand *out*. A hand up is an opportunity, but we must have an opportunity to pay someone back instead of getting something for nothing. We hate being in anyone's debt.

If someone is in need and my spirit tells me to help him or her, then I'll offer an opportunity to them – a project or something that we can co-create. I might say, *"Do you want to mow my lawn?"* or any other odd job.

Helping people in a way that preserves their dignity allows everyone to contribute. Everybody has something to offer. If you give an elderly woman twenty-five bucks to pay her electric bill, and you don't see any apparent way that she can do anything for you except maybe sit there and visit – then let her do just that. Perhaps she can counsel you, tell you a story, or give you a good piece of advice.

Then you can say, "You know, you've already paid me back. By the way, I've enjoyed this visit and the information you've given me. This has been the most enjoyable afternoon. Thank you for sharing your time with me and keeping me in your prayers."

Appalachians are not a people to look down upon, make fun of, or treat with condescension. We're people who need to be respected and acknowledged for our rich culture. We know our strengths result from our spirit. We are stubborn and proud, but we'll accept an opportunity, though if you want to offer us something out of obligation or insincerity, then don't bother.

Mountain people have always possessed a keen intuition. Even when outsiders are lying through their teeth, we know the truth and we can sense where they're coming from. I think this way myself. I know if you are not being sincere with me. You can tell me one thing, but I am feeling all the other stuff. We have antennas all over us. We rely on our intuition and know exactly what's going on.

Exploiters have come to the mountains to take advantage of the resources and to disregard the people. However, people are the true resource of the mountains. We resent the way big companies came into the mountains and worked the Appalachian people into the ground, sometimes literally, and then walked off with their sacks full of money. Then they had the gall to justify it through political rhetoric, but still to this day, we are looking for how we benefited from their efforts. My sister, Dolly, has done more to improve the lives of the people in East Tennessee than anyone else I can think of in the last fifty years through job opportunities and educational awareness. However, you can't judge the rest of Appalachia by East Tennessee because it is a major tourist destination these days.

Fortunately, we mountain folk are resourceful. We can take the tragedies and turn them to our advantage. Our modest homes may not be a five-star resort hotel like the Greenbrier in West Virginia, but in Appalachia, we'll let weeds grow back up and those weeds will turn into beautiful wildflowers. Nevertheless, we'll make the most of what we have and be thankful for it as we always have. Our children will grow and we'll thrive, and God will love us, and the sun will shine, and the sky will be blue over Appalachia, despite the abuse and neglect.

The proud and stubborn heritage of our Scot/Irish ancestors is still alive and well today in our beloved mountains. Wonder what it must have been like for those who came from Scotland and Ireland. They were poor and outcast in their own country. They left their homeland in search of a better life and a chance for freedom and prosperity. But the lack of an education and meaningful employment has continued to plague us. Gradually, I see changes but we still have so far to go.

When I was about seven years old, some tourists came driving into our holler. We didn't even own a car at the time. A woman and her children came driving through looking at us as if we were exhibits at a zoo. We were little dirty-faced mountain urchins playing on the bank behind trees. As they drove slowly by, we could hear her say, "Oh, look at the little mountain children, honey." I felt like we were being regarded as mountain goats or monkeys. I grew angry about her comment, and I resented her. As a matter of fact, I hated her for it because even then, as a child, I had my Appalachian pride.

We couldn't afford store-bought bedding when I was growing up, and since some of us were bedwetters, we would have ruined it anyway. Instead, my mother would make these mattress ticks. She would sew pieces of fabric together until it was as big as a full sized bed, and then she would stuff it with straw. That's what I slept on for most of my childhood. I loved hearing the sound of that straw. It's great for sleeping because it sounds like rain.

I can never forget sleeping on a straw tick covered with homemade quilts, and feeling grateful to have them both. Sometimes two of us would sleep at the head and two would sleep at the foot of the bed just like that Little Jimmy Dickens song, "Sleeping At The Foot Of The Bed." There would be four of us kids snuggled in the bed like a litter of puppies just to keep ourselves warm. Looking back, I appreciated what I had, but I love what I have now.

Sometimes these days, I have the good fortune to ride in the back of a limousine, yet as a child, we didn't even have a car to drive. What a contrast! But to this day, I find I'm more comfortable in the cab of a pickup truck than in the back of a limousine. I will never forget where I come from. As long as the room is warm, I would also be comfortable and as much at home on a straw tick. I don't like sleeping in cold rooms though. While growing up in those cold Appalachian winters, I experienced enough of that for a lifetime.

When I get to stay in nice places, I can't help but be reminded of other children in Appalachia sleeping on straw ticks or maybe no bed at all. We had no indoor plumbing ourselves. We had no telephone service until I left home. Until I entered high school, indoor plumbing was only a dream.

By sharing some of my own experiences, I hope there will be those of you who understand that it makes no difference how far back in the race you start. Just start. What matters is that you always believe that you're a winner. Because it ain't over 'til it's over.

What a miracle it is that I've been able to go from sleeping on a straw tick to a two-sided mattress with a thermostat-controlled electric blanket and a down comforter. I count my blessings when I see homeless people panhandling or hear of people freezing under a bridge. Coming from where I came from, it is never far from my mind that it could be me on the street or freezing under a bridge – it could be any of us.

Never take your blessings and your prosperity for granted, because you are no more special than anyone else. We have our blessings so that we can share them. There's always some way we should be trying to help someone else. The most important way to do this is to have compassion and to love those less fortunate. Many have shown me compassion and I'm thankful, but simply being thankful is insufficient. I have to pass it on and so should you.

When I was ten, I contracted hepatitis. I was very sick, but my parents couldn't afford to put me in the hospital. My mother took me to see the doctor who had a big loud-mouthed nurse working for him. She made me pee in this little potty, and that embarrassed me to no end. After I finished, the nurse came in, picked up the potty and, as she left the examining room, I heard her yell down the hall, "Yes, sir! Pure gold!"

I was so embarrassed that she had remarked about my urine being so yellow and all. I was a very modest child. I was living in a small house with many children, and modesty became the norm. The girls slept on one side of the house and the boys on the other. Modesty was just a way of life with us. It was actually a by-product of our cramped living conditions, but also a reflection of my parent's values. We were brought up with total respect, decency and love from our parents and for each other. When some people hear about our small house with so many children, they automatically make innuendos about sexual improprieties occurring. I find that so offensive, not only to me, but also to the values my parents tried to instill in us.

Anyway, at the hospital, they examined me without my shirt and pants on. The doctor pushed around on my stomach with his hands. I was sick enough to die with hepatitis, but it took my mother, that big loud-mouthed nurse, another nurse and the doctor to hold me down to get my clothes off. Modesty can be powerful at times. The doctor insisted on admitting me to the hospital, but my mother told him they couldn't afford it and that she would just have to take me back home to recuperate.

As we drove home from Knoxville after my embarrassing examination, we decided we'd better stop at my Aunt

Exa's grocery store so Mama could call Doctor Thomas. She told him I was suffering from hepatitis, and asked him if he would mind coming to check on me. He was quite elderly by this time and should have been retired. By now, he was traveling in a car and every three or four days he drove over to examine me to make sure I was okay. That same missionary-doctor-minister also oversaw the Methodist Association's distribution of Christmas gifts and extra food. What a special man he was.

I consider Doctor Thomas a missionary because he was a minister and a doctor who had moved to our little community of Pittman Center and opened a clinic. He delivered my four older siblings. He would ride his horse to our house and to other homes, deliver babies, and take care of those who were sick. I was born at a clinic in Sevierville, as were the next three of my siblings. An Army doctor delivered us. (The clinic of my birth is now the health department.) The last four were born at Baptist Hospital in Knoxville.

When I was growing up, the Methodist Church organization had a fine program in our part of the Appalachian Mountains. Other groups were also represented – like the Christian Appalachian Project that's headquartered in Kentucky. A Catholic priest, Father Ralph Bieting, founded it 50 years ago. When I work with them, it makes me think about Doctor Thomas and his missionary efforts in the mountains of East Tennessee.

More missionaries and church organizations need to do more work in the Appalachian Mountains. It's good that we have missionaries who go out of the United States and help people in other nations, but Appalachia needs a lot of help. It's similar in its need to the inner cities across our country. Although we have better hospital facilities, telephones, and better roads in some areas, more could be done. Job and educational opportunities are still very lacking. Some people are still living so far below the poverty line; it may be generations before they catch up to modern standards. The housing for some is just as bad as it was a century ago. I invite our government officials to take a drive through Appalachia with an open mind. Most of these people would love to work if they had a job and an education to help them provide for their families. When I came down with hepatitis in 1959, the doctor came and looked after me free of charge because of our poverty. In certain areas of Appalachia, the situation hasn't changed one bit but it seems the charities look outside the country now.

Sometimes we bartered for services. Daddy paid Doctor Thomas a sack of meal to deliver Dolly. She was an expensive baby. Sometimes we'd pay him with chickens, or whatever we had available for bartering. And he took it because he was poor as well. But that's what it was like. He was there to do God's work. And God's work he did.

Those country doctors were angels. There weren't any specialists – they did everything - delivered babies, dealt with internal problems, performed surgeries, and treated illnesses of every kind and every catastrophe that came along. Doctor Thomas cared for me when I was sick and had hepatitis and also came and checked on all the other children and gave them immunizations so the rest of the household wouldn't come down with it. Those country doctors were definitely angels in my life and in the lives of so many other mountain children.

Every good parent wants to give his or her children everything. My relatives were no different. They were proud people. They provided with what they had available to them, but we never went hungry. We always had our own home, and Daddy made sure we had plenty of wood or coal to heat our house. My Aunt Nell, who was actually my Aunt Estelle's sister-in-law, and my mother's two sisters saw to it that we had clothes to wear. I loved to smell those boxes those clothes came in and I would imagine what the little girl looked like who had so many clothes that she could give some of them away.

I didn't mind wearing hand-me-downs. I was grateful for the opportunity just to prowl through those boxes of old clothes collected from the wealthier people in Knoxville at the Catholic Church. However, pain came from being made fun of by the children in school. As I think about it, growing up poor is a blessing. It teaches you compassion for others.

I never missed what I didn't have though. What bothered me about the way we grew up was that my dad worked really hard all the time and my mama was always sick. My older brothers and sisters remember when Mama wasn't sick, but from the age of five until I left home at fifteen, Mama was sick most of the time. This was a struggle for me since I was the oldest girl still at home.

At times, I feared that Daddy might leave us because things were so bad - so dreadful at times, I wondered why he didn't leave, and all the while praying that he wouldn't. I worried about being abandoned many times as a child.

Teachers weren't wealthy, but compared to us, they were extremely high on the "gettin' pole." When I was in the fourth grade, I was so happy one morning to wear a new little outfit my Aunt Christine had given to me, a hand-me-down from her daughter, Marjorie. It was a cute little white-collared blouse with tiny pink flowers on it. I put this outfit together with little pink pedal pushers (they call them Capri pants now). Oh, I was so proud of myself. I went to school early that morning because I was so happy to have new clothes. I *knew* I looked pretty. Willadeene, my oldest sister, had even let me have a dab of her Blue Waltz perfume behind each ear.

I sat in the hallway by the classroom door waiting for my teacher. There were other children around. Another teacher walked by and stopped when she saw me. In a loud voice that everyone could hear, she said, "Well, now look at you, Stella, you have on clean clothes." My blood turned to ice water in my veins.

I really think she was trying to compliment me, but I was devastated that she thought of me as someone who normally wore dirty clothes. What I wish she could have said was, "What a pretty little girl you are today, Stella, you look beautiful." I hated that teacher after that. For her to say that really hurt.

Having my stubborn mountain pride, I would have died before I would cry and I would have died before I would let her know I cared. The other children quickly noticed it, so my entire excitement and joy was stolen from me by someone's ignorance. I still feel like crying today when I think about how it destroyed me at the time. She stole some of my innocence. A child's innocence is irreplaceable. Early wounds are deep ones. Frequently they never truly heal. Just look at me! It's been a hard-won lesson, but I've learned that you can't take things personally.

As you grow, you learn to prevent others from robbing you of your joy. That teacher was really quite silly, to do that to me. Unfortunately, she was just incapable of communicating with a child, I suppose. She failed to realize my sensitivity and to respond accordingly. Just because I was poor didn't mean that I was not intelligent; it didn't mean that I was without pride, it didn't mean that I was without dignity, it didn't even mean that I wasn't sensitive to the bone. I was all of those. That same teacher is very old today and I have come to see she meant no harm.

Although such an event can affect people for life and destroy their self-esteem, I have kept it from happening to me through my spiritual life.

None of us ever gets it all figured out. Life is a great adventure, and I'm "just so proud to be here," as Minnie Pearl would say. In the end, I don't care what others think. It's most important what I think of myself.

Others laughed at us because we were "hillbillies." I've spent a lot of energy throughout my life hoping to be accepted. Often I wasn't. Most of us know the feeling of rejection I'm sure.

Ridicule, rejection and poverty is something that affects you all your life. I've traveled enough to know that there are rednecks and jerks everywhere. Ignorance is chronic to humans the world over. I'm proud to be from the Appalachian Mountains.

I'm proud to have been raised by loving, spiritual parents. I'm proud to have ten full brothers and sisters and a half-brother and half-sister.

Now, if anyone would know anything about rejection, *I* would - growing up in Nashville, trying to survive in the music business, and having many doors slammed in my face. My peers and the industry leaders disregarded my artistry because Dolly's career has been so phenomenal. Dolly's success being so tremendous and people judging *my* success by *her* success could have destroyed me. Dolly and I are very different in many ways. I would never have been comfortable with the public image my sister has enjoyed. Yet, everyone has something to overcome – whether it's cold and unloving parents in a wealthy environment, or the ravages of poverty or being unfairly judged and rejected, not to mention some folks' health challenges.

I try to be the best Stella I can be. If I can do that, then my life is one more miracle that I can enjoy. I hope that I can be a blessing to someone else.

But God definitely does live in these mountains here among those of us who love Him. I'm now working with the Christian Appalachian Project. They need money to help the poor here in Appalachia. We need money for education. We need industry. But most of all, we need what we've always had, and that's God's love.

Many leave the place they're from, change their accent and try to forget their roots. Not me - I left the mountains, but the mountains never left me. I'm proud to say, "I am from the Great Smoky Mountains. I am an Appalachian child. I'm a mountain woman." Maybe I've grown a little worldly and a little more sophisticated being out in the world, but I will always have a mountain woman's spirit. That means I take care of my family, and myself.

Over the years, I often ask those I meet where they come from, and I practically have to wring it out of some of them. That's not true with Appalachian people. They just come right out and tell you where they're from and they're all proud of it. Wherever in the world they go, they'll let you know very quickly where they're from. This demonstrates a pride born in us that will live in our hearts forever. We love our land, our mountains, and our home.

I always go back to the mountains to nourish myself in the woods and to walk in the hollers and on the hills - where I feel the healing spirit of God.

You may say, "Stella, that's just going home – and that's the nurturing of home." Yes, it is, but it's like a vitamin shot to go back to the mountains and feel the security of being embraced and cradled there. Those hills are deep and old, and there's a certain spirit I've never felt anywhere else. Just the way the sun shines on the mountains in Appalachia differs from anywhere else I've been.

I've met beautiful people from all over the world who have good hearts, do the right thing, and believe in goodness. Your home provides only your foundation.

I wrote a note to my son at Christmas reminding him, "Just remember, home is always in your heart. You can make a beautiful, peaceful, loving home or you can make a home full of strife. But no matter where you are, home will always be in your heart." If someone's home is a place of strife, they can change it by trusting enough to surrender to love.

My family members always liked to say there was a big "I" and a little "You" syndrome going on in the world. In other words, outsiders would come in acting as though they were the big people and we were their inferiors. As a child, I would see tourists come to the Smoky Mountains in Gatlinburg, Pigeon Forge and Sevierville, Tennessee. We'd watch them with amazement. To us poor kids, they were rich people. They made us wonder what we could some-day become if we were no longer confined to the hills and valleys and chained to poverty. Later, I realized that most of them were not extremely wealthy or sophisticated travel-ers – they were just your average middle class tourists.

The point is not about where you're from, although that sets your path; it's who you are and where you're going. My sister, Dolly, wanted to grow up to be a star, and I wanted to grow up to be a missionary, and my sister, Cassie, wanted to grow up to be a tourist. Cassie wanted that because she thought tourists wore nice clothes. She knew they must have beautiful houses. I was thinking about it just the other day, we've all gotten our wish or should I say, our miracle.

"It isn't where you come from, it's where you're going that counts."

– Ella Fitzgerald

My First Miracle

My first miracle came at the very early age of five. Outside on the back porch in the freezing cold of winter, my mama was doing the laundry – "the washin'," as she called it. I was playing around on the living room floor when suddenly she came back inside, telling me, "Honey, you need to be quiet because Mama's got a headache. Just come over here and pray for me."

I knew something was wrong, so I prayed to Jesus. Kneeling by her side, as she lay sunken into the sofa, I asked Jesus to make her head feel better. My mother became so ill later they took her to the hospital where she was diagnosed with spinal meningitis. Medical experts gave her up to die.

That entire winter – my grandmother, granddad, aunts, and my dad along with different members from our church – would talk about her not making it. They didn't understand what effect their discussions were having on her children. I remember we were all so frightened because we were about to lose our mother. My aunt would say, "Well, I went by the hospital this afternoon and the doctors said they don't expect her to live through the night." As a five-year-old, I heard this over and over.

Many things were going wrong. Mama had lost her hearing in one ear because of this infection. She also had tuberculosis and my relatives came to the house and said they needed to put her in a sanitarium for a while because of the TB. She remained in the hospital for a long time in very critical condition. And all the while, she was pregnant with my little brother, Larry.

They held prayer meetings every night in our living room, but I had already believed that God would heal her. I had prayed about this to Jesus, and yet she was still sick. With the innocence of a child, I lectured Jesus just a bit. I said, "You *know*, Jesus, I *asked* you to make her head feel better!"

Children back then were taught to be seen and not heard, so I said nothing to the adults because I was just a kid. But I kept saying to myself, "No, they can't put her in the TB hospital."

But God healed her. They all talked about how God had healed her and how all that prayer had worked this miracle.

Well, I *knew* that. I also believed it was *my* prayer that God had answered, not theirs. Even at that age, I was private enough never to share my opinion with any of them. Sure enough, my mother recovered and she finally came home from the hospital on a stretcher.

On a hot July day, she gave birth to my little brother, Larry. He was born with a lung disorder from all the trauma. Although he was a perfectly beautiful baby, he only lived for eleven hours. My mother couldn't attend his funeral because she was still in the hospital recovering from childbirth. I remember crying for her that night as I went to sleep.

It was one of the most sobering experiences in the world of a child – to be five years old and have your mother stricken with a catastrophic illness, and almost die. Hearing from day to day that she might not live through the night was almost unbearable and to experience the death of my baby brother was very traumatizing. His death affected my siblings and me deeply. He was born on July 5, 1955, the ninth member of our family. We still count him as a member of our family – because he was…and is.

Before this happened, that same year, we moved, from one house to another. As we were moving, I had what you might call a precognitive experience – my family members would call it a vision. In this vision, our truck containing all our belongings crashed and turned over while I watched.

Later, the movers came back to pick us up and told us about the accident, the truck throwing all our furniture down a bank off the side of the road. Just as I foresaw. My two older brothers David and Denver had been on the truck, but they jumped out of harm's way in time without injury.

Now, this frightened me because I saw it happen before it actually happened. Because of the doctrine preached in our church, I was afraid to tell anyone. They might think I was possessed. My grandfather was a Pentecostal preacher, and my mother, aunts and all the rest of my family were charismatic Christian people. They spoke in the unknown tongue, laid hands on the sick and prayed for them. They anointed with oil and believed in all the spiritual gifts in the New Testament (I Corinthians 12:1-31). It was not uncommon to hear them speak of people being possessed with demons (Luke 8:29). I worried they might try to cast the devil out of me. I'd heard about people being demon-possessed even at that age.

I never shared the experience with anyone. I was afraid to reveal it for years because I didn't want them to think that I was demon-possessed. Later, as a teenager, I would play mind games with my sisters Dolly and Cassie. I continued to have visions like the accident on moving day, but I never said a word about them except to my sisters.

As I grew into an adult, I had more experiences of the same sort. I saw things before they happened. I later learned it was called having "the sight," that is what the elders in the mountains called it. Reading numerous books about it, I realized I had a gift. I've studied the Bible since I could first read. Later I learned about other religions, and studied every book available to me on the subject – New Age and all.

The more I read, the more I realized that we all have gifts. I make a living with one of mine – singing. I believe all gifts must be used very thoughtfully and carefully. Sometimes they are wonderful things to have; often times they can be a burden.

My life started this way. My earliest memories of spiritual things go back to the age of five.

I was too young to have any idea of what I was going to have to deal with. As a child, you live from moment to moment, sensation to sensation, day to day. You see the world and your life as infinite.

At my little brother's funeral, I saw him in his tiny casket at the funeral home. He looked like a little angel, so perfect as far as I could see. I wondered: Why did he die? Yet, I never asked anyone the question. I asked only myself. I just remember the smell of the flowers and the dirt at the gravesite when they lowered his little coffin.

Such experiences affect a child greatly. You don't quite know how to analyze them, at such a tender age. You only know how to react to things. If you're analytical, as I think

I've always been, as you grow, you analyze such traumatic events over and over. You seek information to help you piece together a coherent picture of powerful events that make you who you are.

That may explain why I've always been an avid reader. My curious mind always leads me to read books on psychology. I wanted to understand human behavior, I guess. We often try to be very scientific and pragmatic, but how can I explain scientifically that I had precognitive experiences at five years of age? Can some brain scientist or world-renowned intellectual explain it to me? I am not so sure.

I never doubted the power of the spirit world. I always relied on the spirit – my spirit - because I know what happened to me. It's not something someone needs to tell me. At other times, I feel that I have protectors, angels as it were – earth angels. I do not necessarily believe that celestial beings help me, but angels here on earth have assisted me in times of trouble many times throughout my life.

I used a CB radio back in the seventies before cell phones became popular. I cannot tell you how many times Christian truck drivers and other travelers would assist me over the CB radio into and out of towns, sometimes for hundreds of miles. Keeping me awake, helping me locate places I was working and even stopping and looking after me while I filled my gas tank and bought food. Then they would fade into the night as if they had appeared just for my needs.

On the road alone, – a young woman traveling in a car – I sure needed help from time to time. Ghosts – no. Angels – yes.

"The job of parents is to guide, not to own. Our children are not ours."

– Suzanne Somers

The Doll That Became My Son

There were many more miracles after the one I experienced at the age of five.

My next miracle occurred at the same tender age. In 1955 I received a doll for Christmas, a little rubber doll with shoes and socks and clothes molded into the rubber. My doll, made by the Sun Rubber Company in Cincinnati, Ohio, was called Toddle Tim, and I loved it.

At that point, I decided that when I grew up, I would have a little boy and I would name him Tim. I told everyone of my plans as I grew older.

When I would lose my doll, mama would say to the kids, "Lord, young'un's, get out there and help Stella find her Timmy doll or she'll be crying all night." All my brothers and sisters would scurry out into the weeds around the house and help me find my doll. Sometimes the dog would carry it off, but it never chewed it up. I guess the rubber was just too hard.

The doll is still in good shape, and I treasure it. It's my Timmy doll. I showed it to Tim's friends at his thirty-third birthday party in November of 2001. Let me tell you, he really loved that – not one of my smarter moves.

Reading from the Bible, I realized that Timothy was a wonderful person, but mostly I just loved the sound of that name. I knew my son would grow up to be a good person and a fine man just like St. Timothy and that made it all the more perfect.

Sure enough, when I was nineteen years old I had Timothy. I don't know how I had known this would happen any more than I knew the furniture was going to be thrown off the truck during the move. I knew he would be a male child all the time I carried him. I knew how much he would weigh, and what he would look like.

I don't know how I knew it and I can't explain it. It's not as if I'm some fortune-teller or anything. He still has blue eyes and blond hair, and he's *still* a doll, but of course, I'm his mom.

I was a teenager with a baby. I already knew my marriage was in trouble and I would most likely rear this child alone. When they brought him to me and laid him in my arms for the first time, I saw that Tim looked just like the doll. He had blue eyes and blonde hair exactly like the doll. I promised him that I would be a good mother. He looked at me as if to say, "So you're it!" He stared at me and I felt that he was saying, "I'll do my best – I'll be good, Mama." I would do everything I could to give him opportunities in life. I had grown up in a household where my father could not read or write, yet I learned to read and to write and received a high school diploma. Somewhere, I read that education was freedom. I promised my son that I would do everything I could to provide him with an education and the freedom that would bring.

It was indeed a miracle to watch my son walk across the stage at Vanderbilt University and receive his undergraduate degree. It was another miracle to see him walk across the stage to accept his law degree from the University of Tennessee. In addition, it was even more of a miracle when I saw him at the War Memorial Auditorium in Nashville being sworn in by the Tennessee State Bar. That's a lifetime of miracles right there. Sitting there and remembering all the hard work and all the nights of praying and crying. I saw that it had finally paid off with what Tim had accomplished.

The last time Tim and I were at the War Memorial Auditorium; Tim was four years old and had just won the Nashville Children's Pageant. When he was sworn in 25 years later, in the same historic building, his father, stepmother, aunt and uncle were there to watch the proud moment. We sat there for two hours waiting for his turn to come around.

I couldn't help but remember how hard it had been to raise him. Back then it was, "God, please let me have enough money to pay my rent, please make sure Tim's babysitter is looking after him properly. Please don't let Tim get sick while I'm away." I was too independent to ask his dad for help, and his dad was too stubborn to offer.

Nevertheless, Tim visited regularly with his dad throughout his childhood. I never kept Tim away from his dad and his family even though he never contributed financially. I do not think children should be used to punish a parent. I tried very hard to avoid that in our situation, regardless of the circumstances.

Finally, it was worth it, all those years of sacrifice when I saw this beautiful, handsome young lawyer who was the child of my own body walking across the stage.

That's pretty miraculous. I took it as such. Never for a minute did I fail to see the blessing in that special moment passing before my eyes. Tim's birth, growth and life gave wings to the Appalachian lullaby – *Child of My Body:*

Child of my body
My child, my child, my son
You are like your mother
You are, you are
Like no one

Hearts move in all directions
Always reaching, reaching
To the sun
Where, where have you flown to
My angel, my angel, my son

Fly to the heavens
Onward you go
Over stars and rainbows
Your secrets yet to unfold

Take heart in knowing
You came with all you need
Trust in your being
The light you have seen

Child, child of my body
Child, child of my soul

"Child Of My Body"
Written by: Stella Parton
© 1995. My Mama's Music (BMI)

The baby, the child of my flesh, love of my life. I had envisioned him as a five-year-old child myself when I held my Toddle Tim doll to my chest. Now, my living doll is an accomplished and sensitive adult, walking across the stage of life with confidence and charm.

I was caught up in one of the greatest miracles of my life. I give God the credit for every blessing.

"Sometimes it takes years to really grasp what's happened in your life."

– *Wilma Rudolph*

I'll Fly Away

I t is unnatural when children die. I was almost six years old when my cousin, Cordie Ann, died. She and her brother, Carl Gene, were staying with their paternal grandmother when it happened.

Apparently, their grandmother was burning leaves in the front yard. All children love to gather leaves into a pile and roll around in them. I was no different myself and remember doing so in the autumn. Her grandmother lit a pile of leaves. She must have turned her back for a minute to run into the house for something. Cordie Ann's dress caught fire, and her grandmother was unable to catch her and put it out fast enough. By the time she reached her, too much damage had been done. Her death affected me greatly because we were the same age and I just could not understand it.

In the funeral home, her mother was so distraught. Cordie Ann looked so peaceful lying there in her little casket wearing a little pink dress. There was no pain on her face. I remember her soft blonde hair and pink skin with the round cheeks of a child. I saw no burn marks on her. She looked like she was sleeping. I asked my Mom and she said the fire burned her stomach underneath her dress. The water her grandmother had used to put out the fire kept the flames away from her face and hair, but unfortunately, the smoke destroyed her lungs.

I was more confused than ever and horrified at the gravesite when they lowered her little casket into a box inside a deep hole in the East Tennessee clay. We should have been running and playing together on the hillside. My thoughts often ran to those events. Each time we passed by the house where her grandmother lived, I imagined her running and playing in the yard.

That day on the hillside in the afternoon sun, I stood in stunned silence as they placed the homemade flowers made from crepe paper that had been dipped in paraffin days before the funeral on her little grave. I still see my mother's soft short fingers spread out wide to scallop the edges of the crepe paper into different shapes before they were twisted into different colored flowers and dipped into the melted wax. I loved watching my mother be creative even though the motivation this time was a sad event. There were also wildflowers picked from the fields, placed neatly in pint and quart sized fruit jars with water halfway up the side.

My Aunt Dorothy Jo played a guitar and led us in songs as Cordie Ann's mother, aunts and little brother wept. I thought about how it could have been me and how sad my brothers and sisters would be if it had been me instead of Cordie Ann. I hardly heard the voice of my Granddad as he prayed the last prayer over her, thanking God for allowing her to walk on this earth for such a short time and asking God to welcome her back home in Heaven.

Fifty years ago in the mountains, we were without the means to buy flowers from a florist like we do today. We picked them from the yard and fields – wild daisies, black-eyed susans, Queen Ann's lace, wild lilies, rambling roses and so on. Or else we made them with crepe paper. Crepe paper flowers were a true art form before the plastic flowers came along. Mama taught us to make crepe paper flowers as soon as we could use the scissors and a hairpin to shape the crepe paper.

We made dozens of flowers for Decoration Day or Memorial Day as it's called in other parts of the country. Each year, we took flowers to the Martin Graveyard in Greenbrier where Daddy's little sister Marjorie was buried. We also took them to Evans Chapel, Shady Grove and Caton's Chapel because we had relatives buried in each of these cemeteries. Decoration Day was one of the biggest social events of the year when I was a child, but as I matured, it changed and became less important.

Maybe I shouldn't tell you this, but then, again, maybe I should. I'm not ghoulish, but I think it's important for us to understand not only how to live, but also how to die.

For several reasons, I decided that I want to be cremated when I die. I do not want to have a funeral in the conventional sense because funerals are just so overdone and the expense is excessively high. The next of kin are in emotional turmoil, overwhelmed by so many decisions as to the funeral home, casket, visitation, pallbearers, memorial service, and burial plot. I don't want someone having to select some fluffy pink dress for me to wear that is open in the back like a hospital gown.

I'll just make it easy for my family right here and now. I don't want them to go to the trouble, expense and the anguish over me when I am no longer here. There's no way I want to be dolled up with makeup, much less have my body laid out in front of all my friends, family and who knows who else to view. It only makes a dead person look deader and I don't want people looking at me if I can't look back!

Why should my child and other loved ones be saddled with the responsibility of picking out a casket for my body? We come into this world with nothing. Why shouldn't we go out the same way?

I don't want my body rotting in the ground somewhere. A hundred years from now, someone could decide to exhume it and swipe a piece of my DNA to clone me.

Anyway, many folks disagree with this, I know, but I hate burials in the ground. Digging a hole in the earth, shoveling dirt on top of the coffin, often in the rain or in the snow, I don't think so, it's horrible, and I have never liked it. My friend, Maggie, was cremated and it was a lot easier to think of her spirit as free afterwards.

During our lives, I think we make so much out of the wrong things. We spend so much time worrying about making money, becoming successful, and having our friends admire us, we forget to play with our children, our pets or even enjoy a good glass of water. We forget to enjoy a long bath and a good meal. We are so stressed and anxious about being included in some group or organization or church function or work project or whatever that we're just not living our lives to the fullest.

Then one day, when it's all winding down, and we're in the hospital on oxygen, needles plugged into every appendage, we wonder what it was all for. Somehow we let our lives just pass us by and now we're sliding out of this world.

Life is the energy we put out. It's not glorifying ourselves. It's the energies and the intentions we transmit while we're here. *And if Christ be in you, the body is dead because of sin; but the Spirit is life because of righteousness. – Romans 8:10*

"People see God every day. They just don't recognize Him."

– Pearl Bailey

Anointed Children

I am about four years old. My Mama is lying in the bed praying aloud. My older brother, Bobby, and I are playing around on the floor. My sister, Cassie, is a baby and she's in the bed asleep. She sleeps most of the time. The three of us are under the age of six and not yet old enough to go to school.

Mama tells five-year-old Bobby that he must go to the school and get our oldest sister, Willadeene, and bring her home quickly. He is too little to go that far alone and besides, there is a ferocious bull in the pasture that he would have to cut across to get to the road.

So I insist on going as well, and off Bobby and I run. Before we get to the pasture, my dress gets caught in the fence. Bobby doesn't stop to wait for me but continues on and tells me to go back to the house. I stand there screaming my head off. I feel the sweat pop out on my scalp and it pricks like little needles as I cry out to him to wait for me. He climbs through the fence and I see him run to the other side of the pasture before the bull catches him. I watch him go out of sight. Still sobbing, I run back to the house.

Mama is singing "Amazing Grace" softly. She whispers as I come back inside, "Honey, get Mama the Bible from the dresser." I drag a ladder-back chair across the linoleum floor, climb up and retrieve the family Bible.

Struggling to lift it up to her, Mama places it on her stomach. I climb up in the bed and snuggle up to her as she prays and sings softly. Something's wrong because I can see blood all over the bed. I don't know how to ask her about it because I am still just a baby.

I must have fallen asleep because the next thing I remember my Aunt Ora is there and my brothers and sisters are all home from school. My Mama sleeps as the two men in hospital clothes carry her away on a stretcher while my brothers and sisters are crying. I watch as Aunt Ora scrubs the floor under the bed with water and a broom. She scrubs it out the door and off the porch into the yard. I stand there and watch as the dog and chickens peck around in the dirt now wet with the scrubbing water. Aunt Ora shoos them away with the broom.

Bobby doesn't say much. When he does talk, he stutters from the trauma. It is years before Bobby stops stuttering, but once he does, he speaks more correctly than the rest of us. Bobby is sensitive and quiet even now as an adult.

Mama survived the miscarriage. The trauma of the situation made a deep impression on both Bobby and me. This incident is one of the first things I can remember.

It was a miracle that Aunt Ora was visiting my grandparents who lived down by the river. Aunt Ora had a feeling something was wrong and ran all the way to our house to take care of us until Grandma came. I keep talking about "prayer warriors" and my Aunt Ora was one of those. I'm sure she kept praying after Mama lost consciousness. She had "the sight" as well, because apparently, she had a premonition about Mama.

When I was in the sixth grade, my Aunt Ora was diagnosed with Hodgkin's disease. Her oldest daughter, Earlene, and I were in the same room in school. The doctors told Aunt Ora they had to amputate one of her legs. I remember sitting in class the morning she was supposed to lose her leg, praying for her. However, Aunt Ora told the doctors, she'd just keep her leg and that God would take care of her. She was taken to every healing service anyone heard about in the area. She prayed for God to let her live to see her children grown. She did and saw grandchildren by her youngest daughter who was about five at the time she was diagnosed. Miracle? I think so. She had faith and her prayers worked. She's in the medical books today for having lived so long in such an advanced stage of the disease. God had a purpose for her life. That's just a couple of those everyday miracles that abound.

My Aunt Dorothy Jo made a strong impression on me as well. Even now, she happens to be one person I enjoy being around because she talks about God almost exclusively. She has the best attitude and loves everyone she meets. She's seen many miracles in her life. Dorothy Jo has been a traveling evangelist most of my life and still holds revivals. She is about seventy-three now, but she seems ageless somehow. I think her fountain of youth flows from her continuous worship of the Lord and her genuine love for others. She kind of reminds me of what I envision of Jesus with her gentle and loving ways. Having grown up around her has been a real blessing. My earliest memories of Aunt Dorothy Jo were of revivals in a tent. The services were always crowded. She played the guitar, sang her own songs, and preached about the Lord. I would call my Aunt Dorothy Jo an obedient Christian.

One summer, we heard the grown-ups talking about a friend of my grandpa's coming to preach at our church. They were discussing that he was a snake handler. My grandpa discouraged this practice, but he and the preacher had been friends since childhood. Snake handling was an issue of disagreement between them because Grandpa did not agree with snake handling at all and would not allow it in our church.

Grandpa decided he'd let him preach anyway, but there would be no snakes in our church and no mention of it in any of his sermons. My grandma, my mama and my aunts were not too keen on this decision, but they always went along with Grandpa. Well, after the sermon, Grandpa brought the man by our house for a visit. My parents were out on the porch talking when my brother, Bobby, came walking up the steps. Bobby must have been about twelve at this time. He was always quiet until he stopped stuttering in his early teens. He was holding a Tampa Nugget cigar box. Walking up to the visiting preacher, he opened the lid on the box. In his little stuttering voice he said, "I-I-I-I-I br-br-br-brought you a sn-sn-sn-snake to handle if-if-if you wa-wa-want it." Everyone on the porch, including the preacher, jumped into the yard except for Bobby who was still holding the cigar box, looking a bit bewildered. It's a miracle my daddy didn't give Bobby the belt. I think after the confusion died down, Daddy and Mama saw the humor in it. Needless to say, we never got any closer to snake handling than this experience as far as I can remember. It was not allowed in the church we attended.

When I was six, we moved to a farm my Daddy bought. On the property was an old abandoned church building where my brothers, sisters, cousins and I would "play church." The acoustics were wonderful. We had benches, and the pulpit, and even a bell in the steeple. The windows were the only thing that was missing.

We took turns preaching and being song leader. I recall Daddy complaining about it once and Mama promptly telling him that we could be doing a lot worse things than "playing church." So we practiced harmonies, preaching and even held healing services. Oh, we were very serious about our "worship" service. The area underneath the pulpit was perfect for storing our various church paraphernalia such as prayer cloths, anointing oil, a foot-washing pan and a half-gallon fruit jar to retrieve water from the creek behind the church. However, we could not keep the communion Kool-Aid and crackers there because Bobby and all his friends would sneak in and eat them – those heathens!

That summer, Dolly taught Cassie and me to speak "pig Latin." Occasionally, I would add some to my sermons to impress the little kids. *Eezzusjay entway upya onya ethey ountinmay oooutay araypa.* They thought I could speak in the unknown tongue, except for Cassie of course. I dropped the "pig Latin" from my sermons after Cassie threatened to expose me. However, none of the congregation of our little "play church" went away without a purple mustache and an oily forehead from all the healing services and partaking of the bread and wine in the Kool-Aid jar. We also had clean feet from all those foot-washing rituals.

I sometimes think of the sound in that old church. I believe we probably decided to become singers because of the acoustics. Boy, they were good. It's a miracle we had such a great place to play as children.

"Faith can put a candle in the darkest night."
– Margaret Sangster

Family Miracles

I witnessed another miracle when my brother, Randy, was small. He had been diagnosed with a serious heart condition. He had developed an inoperable hole in his heart, and the doctors told us that Randy wouldn't live to be past the age of 12.

Randy heard this spoken of and he was very frightened. My relatives spoke about such things in front of us children. Their philosophy was to tell us the truth – I guess that's where I get it from. They didn't keep Randy's condition from us, so we kids knew that Randy's last day was fast approaching. He must have been around ten at this time.

So one night Randy decided that he just had to be healed. He had been watching Oral Roberts on television praying for people and he saw our relatives – my aunts, uncles, granddad and everybody praying for people. He asked my granddad, "Grandpa, would you pray for me?"

Of course, my grandpa said yes, and he prayed for him. Every so often, Randy would say, "Grandpa, you need to pray for me. Would you pray for me?" Therefore, Randy decided that that was going to be his mission – to be healed. Every Wednesday night he was at the prayer meetings at the church.

One night I was home doing my homework as Randy left for church. Mama was in the middle of one of her long winter depressions and was unable to go with him. After Randy got back from the prayer meeting, he woke up Mama and Daddy and said "Wake up! I need to tell you something. I was healed tonight!"

Mama said, "Well honey, that's wonderful," she lifted her head up off the pillow and said, "Honey, how do you know?"

She sat up in bed and he said, "Get on up Mama. I want to tell you about it."

Both of my parents got up and sat on the edge of the bed. He said, "The reason I know is because I was being prayed for tonight and there was this warm wind that came through my chest. When they stopped praying, the warm wind went on through my chest, so I know I'm healed."

Mama said, "Well honey, that's wonderful. Let's just praise the Lord."

She knelt down on the floor by the bed and gave thanks for Randy's healing. That's the kind of mother we had. That was the end of that. Everybody was satisfied, and there was no big deal to be made of it until Mama decided to take Randy back to the doctor for his checkup.

The doctor was stunned with disbelief. He said it looked like a skin graft had grown over the hole in Randy's heart. There was no explanation. I think that was a miracle. How else could it have happened? There was no surgery. There was no medical reason as to why the skin graft grew over the hole in the heart. It just occurred and it saved his life. That was such a great miracle for us and for Randy.

Randy has grown into a man who's now way past 40. He is the father of grown children. He's never had heart surgery, and he's never been plagued with problems since. He works out and runs about five to ten miles a day. I think he got into fitness because of his heart problem. He wanted to be a strong person physically, and so he is. I know God has a purpose for Randy's life – and I know he's here for a reason.

Floyd and Freida, my brother and sister who are twins, spent a long time in the hospital due to being born prematurely. Floyd had a collapsed lung, which frightened us because we had lost Larry just two years earlier from the same condition. Finally, after several weeks in incubators, the twins were strong enough to come home. They had many problems those first few years. When they started to walk, they were fitted for leg braces because their legs were weak. Their braces were made of steel and leather and went from their waists all the way to special fitted shoes. To pick them up was almost impossible without being pinched and bruised, not to mention the added weight and awkwardness. I was still a small child. I don't believe I had yet turned eight years old, so it was a struggle to carry them around. The doctors said they would need to wear those braces for several years to help them develop properly.

One day when the twins were about three years old, we heard that a preacher friend of my granddad's was coming to run another revival. The twins decided that if Randy could receive a healing for his heart condition, and Mama could receive her healing for spinal meningitis, then why couldn't they? As soon as the twins saw the preacher coming up the road, they asked for prayer, and he knelt down in the little dirt road in front of our house and prayed for them right there on the spot. A few weeks later, at a regular check-up, the doctors told us they didn't need the braces any longer. Strangely enough, they seemed to be doing fine. Floyd and Freida have both grown up to be very healthy. They are in their forties now, and I don't recall either of them ever complaining about leg, hip or knee problems.

When my brother, Denver, was in his late teens, he had a serious car accident. He broke his neck and spent many weeks in St. Mary's Hospital in Knoxville, about forty miles away.

Mama and Daddy couldn't visit him often because of the distance. Daddy worked, and Mama could not tolerate the stress of this along with all her own health problems and having so many other children still at home. I was about fourteen at the time, so I stayed with my brother as much as possible. I kept him company, since he was in traction with his head in a metal frame. I fed him, scratched him, and read to him. I tried to care for him the best I could to relieve his discomfort. Some days my Grandma Owens would come and relieve me, and I recall how she would always pray for God to heal him. I remember how she lovingly talked to Denver about "living right" as he was the most rebellious of all her grandchildren. He had brought this ordeal upon himself through his own actions. We all suffered seeing him in such a terrible shape. Eventually, he recovered and he never got into as much trouble as he had before.

My grandmother got him through this as no one else could have. God used my grandmother as an angel in my brother's life. Denver was lucky to have had such a special grandmother and so were the rest of us.

More recently, my sister Rachel's daughter Hannah was diagnosed with childhood leukemia. The diagnosis devastated all of us. We had no idea how to deal with watching one of our children possibly die from a catastrophic illness. We sat around and tried to figure out how we could get a bone marrow transplant if we needed a match. In a clan like the Partons, there should be a match somewhere, we thought. The day of her diagnosis, five of us girls were in the hospital with my sister Rachel. The doctor asked Hannah, "Which one is your mother?"

"Well, I have a mother and five others," she answered. I thought what a beautiful remark. That's what family is supposed to do – be there in situations like this. To Hannah, we were the backups for her mother. That's the greatest thing about being family.

We all cried a lot, and we all prayed a lot. Hannah was on every prayer request list across the country. Anyone we knew, who had a prayer chain, had her on it. Each day dad would drive over to our lifelong family friends, Ila and James Parton, and the three of them would pray together for Hannah.

One day, as I drove down the road with my son Tim, I was so upset, grieving for my sister and the potential impending loss of her only child. I knew how it would feel if I should lose Tim.

Tim said, "Mom, I don't know why you're crying so. Why can't you just be thankful for the time we've had her, in case we don't get to keep her."

There he was, my child, rebuking me for my selfishness. I started immediately to be thankful and to pray for a miracle.

God answered our prayers and she went into remission. Hannah's now a beautiful and healthy young woman.

We should listen to our children because they are such great teachers.

My sister Cassie called one day telling me that they believed that her daughter, my niece, Rebecca had cancer in her leg. It was a tumor the size of an egg. She told me they were going to operate immediately.

Once again, we all gathered at the hospital. And once again, I started calling prayer groups I knew. I'm one of these emotional people; I just cry and cry for no reason, so if I have a reason I really cry. I just couldn't bear to look at my sister when they wheeled my seven-year-old perfect little niece down the hall, knowing she may come back without her leg. Earlier, I had accidentally walked into the wrong room and observed the X-rays. I saw the black spot the size of an egg in her leg. And I thought, "Where will they take her leg off? How far will they have to go up to get to the cancer?"

All we could do was pray, and pray some more. It was hard to sit there with my sister, not knowing if her baby was going to come back without a leg, and not knowing what the prognosis would be. We could do nothing but pray. I'd leave the room, and I'd pray. Then I'd return and look at Cassie and I'd break down and start crying again. It would have been better for me to stay in the chapel praying, because I couldn't bear to look at Cassie. It just broke my heart. Her pain caused me pain. Cassie didn't cry – I think she was in shock.

After what seemed like an eternity, the doctors came in and told us the problem was a hemangioma – which is a large collection of blood vessels. Rebecca must have been born with it. They believed that as she grew, it would shrink. Further surgery was not necessary. After they took the stitches out, within a week you could hardly see the incision they made. Here we were, being faced with the possibility of going through a horrible situation and, thank God, it never happened.

I truly believe prayer was answered in these situations.

Many people think entertainers are immune to trauma, illness, death, rape, domestic violence, betrayal and strife. However, it's not true. We all suffer with this or that, day in and day out. We all have our ups and downs, but God gives us hope through faith and through the gift of prayer. Even if things don't turn out as we would hope, we must maintain faith and trust. I myself have lost fifteen people who were very close to me in the last year, but with each one of these losses, I came to a great understanding and great joy in knowing that nothing is forever except the love of God.

Awhile back, a friend came down with testicular cancer. The tumor grew to the size of a grapefruit. He came by my house one night and I knew something was wrong with him. I wondered what it was because I noticed a difference in him from the time I had seen him the week before.

Something noticeably big and unusual was in his groin area. I saw it through his exercise shorts, under his shirt. Obviously, there was a problem. He told us it had grown gradually over the months, and then suddenly its growth had accelerated to the size of a grapefruit. And the pain!

After he left, I told a mutual friend there was something seriously wrong with him and that we needed to pray. I was certain there was a major problem – and I believed it was cancer. Sure enough, he was diagnosed with cancer. They removed a testicle and didn't know what the outcome would be, so they put him through radiation treatments. It was a horrible time for him and for us because he's a very good friend. We kept praying.

Months went by before he had to go back for his checkup. We prayed and believed the whole time that God would take care of him. He called us and told us the exact time he was going to see the doctor to find out what the test results would be. I went into my room to pray because I just wanted to intercede on his behalf. Later, a friend came into the room and said, "Stella, you can get up now. He's just called from the doctor and they say he's cancer-free. There's no cancer."

He still lives a perfectly normal and healthy life.

Thank goodness, God really blessed me with great health through the years. I've had a few scary situations, but mostly I'm steady as a rock. And I pray it stays that way. Whatever happens, we have to go through the experiences of our lives and try to understand them for what they are. If we're to be an example in some way, we can choose to be a good example or a bad example. We also need to be thankful for every day of good health.

As I think about this miraculous life, all the joy, and the pain, I realize how unique my life has been up to this point.

"The best time to make a friend is before you need them."
– Ethel Barrymore

True Love, True Angels

Weeks before Christmas, we used to sit on the hill by our house. We knew Fletcher was coming in his green Chevrolet pickup truck loaded with baskets of fruit, candy and Christmas presents. To us, Santa Claus was a man named Fletcher who wore overalls and drove a green pickup truck.

I'll never forget the beautiful gifts Fletcher brought us. I loved the books most of all. When you're poor, the neatest things seem to be the smallest things.

You can't imagine what it's like to smell a box of crayons and to have a coloring book of your own unless you grew up the way I did. How wonderful to breathe in the aroma of those oranges and apples; just to dig into those boxes of red and white striped peppermint candy sticks; just to get a present. It wasn't things like dolls – it was mostly books and coloring stuff, and educational items. That's one of the things that made us love books so much, other than just our general curiosity. The fact that they arrived in such a magical way made them even more exciting.

We would take turns being the "lookout" for Fletcher's arrival. This went on for days until one of us spotted his green pickup and rushed back to the house with the happy news. "Here comes Fletcher!" we would yell at the top of our lungs when we saw him. That was a wonderful experience.

I'll always be grateful for those generous people. No one ever grows up without help. No one should feel immune to the joy of giving. Fletcher had grown up poor. He was a chubby little man and he wore overalls – I just remember his big stomach and I thought, "Well, he's not really in a red suit, but he still looks a little like Santa." It must have given him such pleasure to watch the excitement on our faces when he handed down the bushel basket of food with the toys in it, and us children reaching up for it.

My dad never learned to read or write but he raised a family of eleven children. We were never on welfare or disability and he never stayed out of work for any reason except for a death or medical emergency. My dad always worked about three jobs – his construction job, a tobacco crop, raising livestock, corn, hay and a garden of enormous size.

The year the twins were born, Daddy had so many bills to pay. One winter night, after Daddy got home from work, two men showed up at our door. They were dressed in suits and ties. They informed Daddy that they were going to garnish his paycheck. Mama had to tell him what the word meant after they left. We all learned what it meant the next payday. Daddy never broke stride. Just like a racehorse, he went back to the job the next morning. That's Appalachian pride at its finest.

But friends like Fletcher pitched in to make a big difference in the world of wide-eyed, excited kids at Christmas time.

Christmas time was never an enjoyable season for my parents, especially my Mom. I believe the financial strain it put on them was the root of their displeasure with the season. Usually Daddy took our tobacco crop to the market a week or two before Christmas. The money from its sale held us over until the weather cleared up in March.

The quality of our Christmas was entirely dependent upon how well Daddy did at the tobacco market. Mama dreaded the holidays because Daddy always stopped off and "had a few" before coming home to tell her how well he had fared at the tobacco market. Mama always feared someone would knock him in the head or shoot him, taking all the tobacco money in the process. But Daddy just couldn't resist stopping off to celebrate with the guys. That regular occurrence usually kept her on edge the whole time he was gone. She just dreaded his coming home "high as a Georgia pine" from celebrating his fine haul.

Mama never liked Daddy to be drunk in front of his children either; although, he was never abusive to any of us in this condition, he would mouth off to her sometimes, which didn't help things. I grew to hate seeing him stagger through the door in the middle of the night drunk. Holding my breath, I feared he would snap and hit Mama. He did a few times. One time was too many in my mind.

When I was five, I had the best Christmas I can recall of my childhood. That was the year I got my "Timmy" doll. At the time, Daddy was attending church and tried his best to live right without alcohol. Daddy's struggle with alcohol affected every one of us in a very negative way. Just the smell of alcohol on his breath when he came home drunk was intolerable. I would usually run and hide until one of my sisters came looking for me. Daddy usually started cursing and crying and wanting Mama and his girls to sing to him. I hated those evenings lined up like stair steps singing for my drunken Daddy as he cried and cursed and swore that Mama could sing a hell of a lot better than Kitty Wells and we were a damn sight better than the Carter Sisters.

Mama prayed for fifty years for Daddy to stop drinking, and when he finally stopped, she had to adjust because he was like a new man. Fortunately, Mama read the Bible through for Daddy those last few years they lived together. He must have loved sitting there in matching recliners listening to the voice of the woman he had loved since childhood, reading the word of God to him. Once, during this time, I called home and Mama was complaining about Daddy. I was in Al-Anon at the time, a support group for children of alcoholics, so I knew what she was going through. She was having withdrawal from not being his "caretaker." So I laughingly said, "Mama, be careful what you pray for, now look what you've gone and let the Lord do for you." Of course, I was just trying to make light of the situation.

One Christmas when I was nine or ten, Mama forgot to buy a Christmas present for me. She had been sick and only felt well enough to go to town the day before Christmas. With twenty whole dollars, she bought ten kids Christmas gifts. As each person opened their gift, she was suddenly shocked when she realized that she had left me out. So she ran to the bedroom and wrapped a gift one of my sisters had received at school. I pretended that I didn't notice, even though I was hurt a little bit. Ultimately, my concern was for her feelings.

We didn't receive many toys for Christmas when I was a child. Usually it was one toy each and they were quickly ruined because there were so many of us playing with them. The store bought toys were cheap and they never lasted more than a week. The things I remember the best are the toys my parents made with their own hands, such as Mama's corncob dolls.

We learned to be creative I think because we lived so close to nature. As a child, I spent hours in the woods making playhouses, carpeting the floors with moss. My parents were creative as well. My Daddy would build things, buy property, fix it up, clear the land and sell it for a profit. His goal was to make more money so he could take better care of us. My mother was creative when she wasn't ill, which wasn't too often. I've come to realize, she suffered from postpartum depression almost all the time from being pregnant. If she wasn't sick and pregnant, she was suffering with depression after having had the latest baby.

I had my own green shag carpet before it ever came into fashion in the '70s. When I moved to Nashville, one of my first apartments was in a beautiful new complex in a nice wooded area, a two bedroom on the second floor. It had a patio and sure enough, green shag carpet. This was when avocado appliances were in fashion as well. I just loved it. I would often sit there and be so thankful that I had been blessed with enough prosperity to live in this new, wonderful place. I would often remember those carpeted playhouses with moss the same color of my floors.

Until I was nine years old, my mother was either pregnant or getting over being pregnant and depressed. What a life for her! And imagine what a life for her children! I don't think people should have more children than they're able to take care of. When I was seven, my 16-year-old sister Willadeene married and left home. My sister Dolly started singing on radio and television and lived with an aunt about 30 miles away. She was gone every holiday, weekend and summer vacation. She was ten at the time. I was the next oldest girl. I was in the second grade when I became mainly responsible for the entire household of eight people until I left home at 15. My responsibilities included helping raise my younger brothers and sisters. There were five younger than I was plus three older brothers. I did most of the cooking, cleaning, laundry and childcare. I felt abandoned by my two older sisters. I never knew a time I did not feel responsible for others.

"Women whose eyes have been washed clear with tears get broad vision."

– Dorothy Dix

Innocence Lost...

The summer I turned fifteen, I spent most of my time taking care of my parents' entire household. Mama was in the hospital with one of her many "breakdowns." When she returned, she was back in bed with her head covered and a new prescription for nerve pills. I had grown to resent her over the last ten years I lived at home. She had been sick or near death's door since I was five. As a result, from the age of seven, I was forced to take on the responsibility of the household and the five younger children. I resented Daddy too. He either worked or disappeared for the weekend to go out drinking with his friends. My parents had unhealthy patterns that the rest of us had to endure.

When my brother, David, left home to join the Marines, there was no one left to help me or to keep order with my siblings. I could handle the care of the smaller children, the cooking, the laundry and the other household chores, but we needed an authority figure to keep my older siblings in line. David's departure ended that.

One beautiful summer day, I decided to walk to the little country store about a mile away that my great-aunt Exa and her husband, Cleo, owned. We always shopped there on credit, and Daddy paid the bill on Fridays on his way home from work. I loved my Aunt Exa and wanted to see her, and I just needed to get out of the house for a while.

On the way there, I stopped off as usual for a visit with my friend Gena, who had just married Joey, a neighbor boy, and was now pregnant. They lived near the school, which was about a quarter of a mile from our house just past the cemetery. Gena and I had become pretty good friends over the short time she had lived there. She had grown up in the orphanage in town. She seemed excited to have a family and a house to live in even if it was the home of her in-laws. The Wilsons were very kind and I had known them all my life. It was exciting to have a pregnant friend almost my age. Cassie and I checked on Gena regularly, and I think she liked having visits from girls close to her own age.

Joey had always been so nice and one of the cutest boys in our community. When I was in the second grade, he endeared himself to me in a heroic manner. The bell rang for the end of the school day. Everyone made a mad dash for the door and I was knocked down in the stampede. When I regained consciousness, I was lying on a low worktable in a classroom with a wet brown paper towel on my forehead. The teacher and Joey were standing over me. He had picked me up and carried me to the teacher. I had a big lump on my head and a deep gash over my right eyebrow from the rush. From that day on, I looked up to him. I thought he was one of the nicest people I knew in my community. I was happy he had found such a pretty girl to marry. I was especially glad to have her as a new friend.

Anyway, after visiting Gena, I walked on to the store. Aunt Exa was always positive and seemed genuinely interested in what was going on in our lives. She was my maternal grandmother's sister. I'm sure she knew about the struggles my Mom endured, but she never mentioned it. After my visit with Aunt Exa, I started home in the afternoon sun, feeling much better than I had when I left.

About halfway back to my house, I met my cousin, George. The closer he got the more I realized that he was growing into a nice looking young man. George must have been about seventeen. We had gone to school together since the first grade. He had failed a couple of times and was usually in my classroom. At my school, there were two grades in each room. I can't remember if he was in my exact grade or the one above. He was always disruptive in class. The teacher always sent him to the principal or made him stand in the corner or stay in at recess.

He really had no friends, but we tolerated him. We thought of him as the "troublemaker." As I think back on it now, he just craved attention. I remember an instance, when a bunch of us were walking home from school, he took his penis out in front of the group and began to urinate on the dirt road making designs in the dust. The other boys chased him, but he only ran away laughing. He was about eight at this time. The other boys hated that he could outrun them.

After George and I met and talked for a while that afternoon on the road, my opinion of him changed. It was the first and only time I had ever had a one on one conversation with him. As I walked away, I remember thinking maybe George is going to grow up to be a good person after all. I was surprised at how nice he was to me. We had talked for only a few minutes there stopped on the road, exchanging thoughts about work, and the weather, family and my going to high school. He worked for some people on their tobacco farm and had some money of his own. He felt proud of himself and I could see that he was happy. I will always remember walking away thinking about how much he had grown. Unfortunately, my wishes of a better life for him ended that very night.

My new friend Gena's husband, Joey, who was my life-long hero, changed all our lives that night. No one knows exactly how or why, but it happened at the lake. There were two or three other boys involved. Apparently, they tied George to the bumper of a car, stabbed him several times and tortured him in other unspeakable ways before throwing his body in the lake. The next day, he was found floating in the water. No one suspected them. They were so highly regarded. They even helped dig his grave. It was a custom for friends and neighbors to dig graves in our little community back then. It was a day or two after the funeral that one of the boys came forward, admitted the crime, and gave all the details of those involved.

No one ever speaks of it, but a darkness settled over our little community that day. Not long after George's murder, a job opportunity presented itself and I was glad to move away. I took a job at the local dime store in town. I lived with an aunt who had four children to raise on her own. I babysat for her at night while she worked the third shift at a factory. I went home for short visits, but lived with relatives until I married during my senior year of high school.

During that time, I developed anorexia nervosa and lost almost a third of my body weight. When I moved in with my aunt, I weighed 115 lbs. I considered it a compliment when my boyfriend stepped off the plane from Vietnam and didn't recognize me. I thought I had just grown up. When I married in my senior year, I weighed only 80 lbs. I thought I looked good.

No one mentioned my weight loss and I never knew I had a condition until I was about thirty. I saw something about it on a talk show and realized I had all the same behaviors. Fortunately, I was able to correct my own eating disorder. I wonder how many people develop psychological disorders and don't realize it. It's a miracle I could correct my own. Yet, to this day, I still see a fat person when I look in the mirror. Life is filled with trauma of one kind or another. Without my faith and the hope of a better tomorrow, I don't know where I would be. I often think of those without hope or those who have lost hope. Even though I have lost trust in people, at times, I have never lost faith in God.

My cousin, George, was buried in the cemetery on the hillside, my hero, Joey and the other boys, went away to prison, and the community grieved the loss of both young boys, not yet men. I moved away and that summer felt our innocence had been lost.

(Names were changed out of respect for the families.)

"Some sort of silent trade takes place between mothers and children."

– Yuko Tsushima

Goodbye Mama

Mama didn't like winter. I often think my mama was born in the wrong place and time. She passed away December 5, 2003. That was just like her to leave us before the holidays got too hectic. When I think of my Mama, I always see a little girl. Avie Lee Caroline Owens Parton was born on the fifth day of October 1923. She was a child of the mountains, a true mountain woman. She left this world praying and talking to dearly departed loved ones gone on before.

My sister, Willadeene, said our mother spoke with her mama and daddy and her sister Estelle the day she died. She even greeted her brother, Robert Henry, who had passed the week before. Mama was never told of Henry's passing because she was too ill. Yet, in a surprised tone, she spoke his name as if to say, "Henry, I didn't know you would be here already." Oh, that gives me such great hope.

Since her passing in her eightieth year of life, I've tried to collect some of my precious memories of her. No, not mementos just little items of behavior that made her mama – my mama.

As I sat looking out my living room window one day at the big magnolia tree, I could almost see Mama in the March wind that brought a cardinal by. It fluttered there, peeking in on me and left quickly. Cardinals were Mama's favorite bird because of their beautiful red color. Mama loved red above all colors.

I remember her sitting at a little pedal Singer sewing machine. She would hum softly amidst the scraps of cloth lying about. I never understood how she created in such chaos, but create she did! She made clothes from scraps. There were quilts, pillows, purses, curtains and bedspreads. Why, Mama made a complete bedroom set of curtains, spreads, comforters, tablecloths and throw pillows for each of her daughter's first homes. Mine was royal blue silk. I've never had one as pretty as the first set Mama made for me. I still see the sparkle in her big brown eyes when she saw how good it looked with my white furniture.

Mama was always creative in the kitchen and never used a recipe. Even if she had, she would have improved it. That was just the way she did things. Mama made allowances for me, the picky-eater, though she never had the time. She was sensitive to the uniqueness of each of her children. Instinctively, she managed some way to help you work through it. She would say, "Stel, you don't know what you're missing out on. You better try this at least once." Daddy would slip me a Hershey's chocolate bar while everyone else sat around eating watermelon on Sunday afternoons. I guess both my parents acknowledged our special quirks.

I think of the little orange neon swim trunks she made for my son, Tim. When Tim was four, I entered him in the Nashville Children's Pageant. The combination of Mom's trunks and Tim's muscle flexing was the trick. He won and I think the swimsuit competition cinched it for him. She just had a way about her. She knew things other people didn't. Daddy knew this about her and that is why he always ran back to mama after his little shenanigans.

Mama had "the sight," as it's often called in the mountains. Once, when Daddy was working on a job as a ditch digger, Mama had someone take her to the job site. She insisted he leave the job at that moment. Daddy was embarrassed and he told his boss that there was a problem at home. The next day on the job, they told him the deep trench he had been working in had caved in thirty minutes after he left the previous day.

Mama believed God showed her those things and I know nothing to contradict that. None of us ever defied her if she insisted on something. She wasn't pushy or bossy, but if she really felt strongly, we never went against her.

I can still see her pregnant belly in the moonlight through my childhood bedroom window. She would get up in the middle of the night to rub my cramping legs with alcohol or liniment. She always called those horrible leg cramps that woke me, growing pains. I would ask her how long I would have them and she would pray softly, rubbing gently until I fell back asleep.

I can still smell the kerosene lamp as Daddy would light it in the middle of the night. I remember Mama walking around our beds giving us something for the "whooping cough." I must have been about three or four. I only remember the concerned look on their shadowy faces in the middle of the night by the coal oil lamp. I feel Mama's soft warm fingers tuck the heavy musty quilt back up around my neck before blowing out the lamp and going back to bed.

My Mama was happiest when she was creative. She was also happiest when her children and Daddy were underfoot. Daddy was ambitious and rebellious. Mama was gentle and creative. They were like vinegar and oil. Once you shake them, you have a great salad dressing. There was obviously a lot of shaking going on in their relationship, and like vinegar and oil, the shaking was necessary to keep them together.

Mama didn't have closure for my brother, Larry, because she was in the hospital recovering from his birth and suffering from spinal meningitis when he died. I remember she and Daddy discussed it several times. Mama wanted a headstone for Larry and we couldn't afford to buy one. Mama came up with the idea for Daddy to build a form and pour one out of concrete. One Saturday afternoon, Daddy came home from town with a bag of cement and we stood back and watched. He patiently listened and worked as Mama instructed him exactly how she thought it should be. Once it was poured, they sat together in the big swing under the big oak tree waiting for the cement to dry. When it dried to just the right texture, Daddy took out his pocketknife and cut a pencil-sized twig from the oak tree. Trimming it to a sharp point, he handed it to Mama. Daddy stood by her as she carved Larry's name and date on the concrete headstone. The following day after church, they carried it up on the hill and placed it on Larry's tiny grave. Again, we stood back and watched them go through this ritual. It was as if we instinctively knew not to interrupt them until it was finished. Years later, they were able to afford to buy a gravestone with the little lamb on top.

I sat on Mama's hospital bed in her room after she passed, reminiscing about this particular incident. My brother, David, spoke up in his quiet voice and he said, "It's still in the garage." They could not bear to throw away Larry's first gravestone after they bought the new one.

Mama loved remodeling and decorating. Her dad was a carpenter when he wasn't preaching. She loved those times she had grandpa all to herself when they worked on one of her many projects. Daddy would tease her and tell people he didn't know which side of the house to find the front door on when he got home from work. He would go on to say, "Avie Lee and Jake may have the house moved to that other hill before they're finished with all their remodeling." She loved it when he teased her. If Mama wanted a new painting for the wall and couldn't afford to buy one, she just painted one herself. My brother, Floyd, has the only remaining painting she did hanging on his wall. Mama shopped mostly in fabric stores. She liked the bargain table the best because she could use her imagination on the scrap pieces, always making a lot out of the rejected pieces. God does that with us, I believe. Mama believed it and lived it.

I don't know what happened to Mama's quilt rack, but I remember the way she cocked her head on her shoulders and how her hands worked feverishly on a quilt top as she sat by the crackle of the heater on those cold dreary days when she battled to stave off her depression. During her manic highs, she gave us all she could, trying to make up for the times she had lost. Depression *is* like a black dog clawing at the front door. I would almost look for "the dog" as I came through the door after school, never knowing which Mama I would have that evening. It's only now, after I have educated myself on depression that I see what Mama endured.

However, I am most proud of the fact that Mama never lost the little girl inside herself. Even to the very end, she allowed herself that one indulgence of being spoiled and childlike. She expected us to make allowances for her as the years swiftly slipped by. And, as was our way, we all indulged her with every ounce of our love for her, trying so hard to give back what she had so freely given to us.

My parents were both very unique individuals. Anything special my siblings or I possess comes from them. I hope the love will always remain with us. I love you Mama. Goodbye little girl. And when I see a cardinal or a field of daisies, I will think of you and my heart will sing.

music

Happy just to be singing.
(Photo by Gordy Collins. Courtesy of the Attic Entertainment Archives)

Singing at the Ryman.
(Photo by Mark Burgess)

2002 CCMA Mainstream Country Artist of the Year. Me and Susie Luchsinger.
(Photo by Mark Burgess)

2004 CCMA Female Vocalist of the Year Award.
(Courtesy of the Attic Entertainment Archives)

Dolly and Me. The original "Big Hair Sisters."
(Photo by Robert Amico / Courtesy of ABC-TV)

Me, Dottie Rambo and Barbara Mandrell sharing a laugh about sisters.
(Photo by Mark Burgess)

Me and the Queen of Country Music, Kitty Wells.
(Courtesy of the Attic Entertainment Archives)

Performing acoustically at an outdoor show
(Courtesy of the Attic Entertainment Archives)

Former Vice-President Al Gore and Me.
(Courtesy of the Attic Entertainment Archives)

Bobby Bare, Me and Joe Taylor enjoying a laugh at a show.
(Courtesy of the Attic Entertainment Archives)

These are some of my racy photos from the Oui magazine article. These
photos were also used on my So Far So Good *album.*
(Photos by Dick Zimmerman)

Yes, that's my real hair.

*Cooking for family and friends in my favorite
cookware: iron skillets and my wood stove.*
(Photo by Bob Bishop / Courtesy of the Attic Entertainment Archives)

"The quality of your life is measured by the little things."
– *Barbara Braham*

Nothing Easy
About Hard Times

I risked being swallowed up in a business full of unsavory characters and sharks. I owe my survival to faith. Coming out of the mountains so young and so naïve, faith is all that kept me going at times.

When I got married, my husband and I lived in Nashville for a while after his discharge from the Army. Eventually we went back to my hometown, Sevierville, Tennessee where I finished high school. There I gave birth to Tim and began beauty school. Soon after, we moved back to Nashville where I continued my cosmetology training, all the while I kept singing in church, and taking care of my son, Tim.

At one point, things were so bad we lived in a dumpy old motel room from which we were eventually evicted and our car was repossessed. Gosh, we were so broke.

Tim's dad had difficulty assuming responsibilities. He suffered anxiety. He'd been a medic in the Vietnam War at the age of 17. He couldn't hold down a job very long because he had severe anxiety attacks. He'd quit a job and we'd go back to Sevierville to be with his family. Once he even loaded up our things while I was at school and we left when I got home that evening, moving back to Sevierville yet again.

While in cosmetology school, we visited my mom and dad over the Christmas holidays. Tim was several months old at this point. Driving up on the hill, I saw a big black Cadillac with Virginia license plates and a big heavyset man in a black suit and a cowboy hat driving away from my parent's home. I thought to myself, "Who in the world is that? Is that someone from the government?" He looked like Dan Aykroyd wearing a cowboy hat. I wondered, "Why are they coming up in these mountains?"

When we got to the house, I asked Mom, "Who was that?" And she said, "Oh, Stella, that was Earl Dixon and his wife, Mary Ruth, and they're looking for you." Earl and Mary Ruth owned a couple of nightclubs in Alexandria, Virginia, and they wanted me to come and work for them.

Even though I had grown up singing with my sisters, I never really dreamed of being a "star." I preferred singing and writing gospel songs. Yet, many people in our area of East Tennessee thought I was talented and had strongly encouraged me to go to Nashville. Earl Dixon's brother, Fred, had told him I might be a good addition to his night-club band.

I thought, "Going to work for them?" I did not intend to be a country singer. Originally, I wanted to go to Lee Bible College down in Cleveland, Tennessee to become a missionary. But things had worked out so differently. I had impulsively married during my last year of high school over Christmas break. A year and eleven months later, Tim had been born. I finished high school and started cosmetology school when Tim was six weeks old.

Despite my plans, I took the job in Virginia because it was too good to pass up. It was an opportunity for my husband and me to work at the same place. I was going to sing with the band, and my husband was going to be a bartender. That sounded all right with me. I was quite religious and had always been in the church. I had never wanted to sing in a nightclub, or a beer joint, as we called it back in East Tennessee.

Two days after Christmas, we drove to Washington, D.C. in a blinding snowstorm. New Year's Eve night was my first night to sing in this club. I had learned enough songs on the drive up there because I didn't know that many country songs. I had always sung gospel music.

When I walked into the place, I received the shock of my life. I knew the Lord was going to strike me dead for being in a nightclub where they sold alcohol. I finally got used to it though, and we settled into a routine in a nice little apartment. Earl Dixon furnished me a car to drive and a cousin of mine moved up to baby-sit Tim, so we were making money and doing okay. Earl, who had become my manager, was really promoting me, so I decided I would just adjust to the new situation.

I was there about six weeks when, while I was onstage singing, a man collapsed on the dance floor. Apparently, he had suffered a heart attack. We stopped playing and everyone moved out of the way. Someone called the ambulance. The staff and patrons carried him to the lobby. We took a break from the bandstand and I walked out to the lobby to see what was going on.

This man was frightened, thinking he was going to die. He was crying and asking someone to pray for him. I looked around and I thought someone older than me should do it, but no one made the effort. I recalled my granddad, my grandmother, mother and aunts and I remembered them quoting the Scripture that says if you are ashamed of me, I'll be ashamed of you. I thought, "Well, I don't want to ever deny Jesus."

He laid there on the table until the ambulance arrived. He cried for his mother. Obviously, she was a good Christian, and I'm sure he thought if his mom were there, he would be okay. I felt I had no choice. I couldn't have lived with myself otherwise. I didn't make a big show of it.

I quietly walked up, and said, "I'll pray with you and I'll pray for you."

I reached over, took his hand and prayed with him as everyone stood around watching. I was shy and embarrassed with everyone standing around holding beer bottles in their hands. I asked God to touch him and not let him die. That poor man was so afraid.

Finally, the ambulance arrived and rushed him off to the hospital.

Some time later, he came back and thanked me. After that, I realized that I shouldn't be so sad and disappointed about where I was, what I was doing, and why I was there singing country music in a nightclub. I discovered that I could be a blessing no matter where I was. Maybe that was my missionary work even though it was a beer joint. God needs foot soldiers on the streets just as well as He needs choir folks in robes.

I've had many opportunities to speak to people and hopefully inspire them to feel better about themselves. Recently, I had the most incredible experience. I participated in an expression of unconditional love. A woman I know down in Jackson, Tennessee, Diane O'Dell, is the longest living person in an iron lung. A mutual friend had introduced us over the phone a couple of years before. We had gotten close through those telephone chats. She's been in this iron cylinder for over 50 years since having polio at the age of three. She's a beautiful spirit and a beautiful person. Her parents are ordinary people. Her dad worked for the telephone company until he retired. Her mother's a home-maker. Together they have taken care of Diane all these years, and she still lives at home in an iron lung.

Diane is one of those earth angels who teaches us so much about living. She's brilliant, she has written a book, *Blinky – The Littlest Star* and she teaches children. After a half century of living in an iron lung, she still smiles, laughs and loves.

Through the Christmas holidays, a humanitarian friend of mine organized a fund-raising party for Diane in the big convention center at the Jackson fairgrounds. The money being raised would keep her from going into a nursing home in the event her parents became unable to care for her. They're in their mid-70's now and take care of her 24 hours a day. There's just no accommodations made for someone in this situation. Yes, she could go to a nursing home, but would not get the individual attention and care she needs and deserves. Her parents have taken care of her on their own all these years and she is going to need the same kind of care and attention because she needs someone on call whether it's to move her foot or her arms or whatever else she needs inside this confining iron capsule.

Diane won't get that kind of care in a nursing home. If her circulation messes up, the motor cuts off, or someone wasn't there to turn it back on immediately, she could die. The benefit party was to insure that she would have round the clock care for the remainder of her life.

They decorated the center to the max, turning it into a winter wonderland with colorful lights and ice sculp-tures. In the food court, a French chef from the Peabody Hotel in Memphis created ice sculptures and an incredible buffet. More than 1,200 people attended the event, including several other artists who performed.

This was Diane's first and only party she had ever attended outside her own home. To see the love in the faces of her parents and the joy in her face gave me so much inspiration. She inspired all of us that night. It was such a magical moment and I was overwhelmed. Actually, I cried off and on all evening. I thought about her confinement in that iron lung with only her head sticking out all of these years. We are able to get up and walk, ride bicycles, drive cars, get on planes, get on trains, get on ships, do whatever we want. We go out to dinner, go to the movies, play with our children, and play with our dogs. Yet Diane, with all her restrictions has a better attitude than most individuals I've met. What do we have to feel bad about?

What in the world do any of us have to feel sorry for ourselves about? Most of us have created our own misery. Diane didn't create this situation, and she has chosen to be a blessing. I felt so blessed to be a part of Diane's party. It was truly a gift from God.

My son, Tim was my escort. It upset him because I was so emotional. All I could think of was how much I love Tim, and the unconditional love between a parent and child. And how many hours, days, months, and years those parents have been on call for the baby they brought into this world through the unconditional love of God. God has empowered them with the supernatural energy to do this job for their child.

Paul Harvey, the well-known radio commentator, did a big piece on Diane. As they wheeled her in, her parents escorted her and the voice of Paul Harvey came booming through the room with the radio report he had made on Diane. Big video screens showed different people talking to her, saying how they wished they could be there for her.

Vice-President Al Gore and people from all walks of life were there for Diane's special night. What a magnificent evening! What a miracle that she was able to enjoy it. What a story, and how blessed am I that I could even attend? She asked for me.

The whole city of Jackson and a lot of others pitched in to make it an incredible event. It was more special to attend Diane's party than to go to a Presidential inauguration ball or a coronation for a queen. This was a coronation for a beautiful princess.

I was an emotional wreck. I realized that I was there for a purpose and Diane was there for a purpose. Diane taught us all how to be a little more thankful for what we have.

You should have seen her face that night. She looked like an angel.

I draw from the well
I just draw from the well
Of God's living water
I draw from the well

My troubles are washed away
Yes, my troubles are washed away
When I draw from the well
I draw from the well

"I Draw From The Well"
Written by: Stella Parton
©2000 My Mama's Music (BMI)

"If your experiences would benefit anybody, give them to someone."

– *Florence Nightingale*

What Goes Around Comes Around

I will never forget when Mothers Against Drunk Drivers approached me to sing their 10th anniversary song. I volunteered to produce the recording and called a bunch of my musician and singer friends. Another friend donated the studio time and engineered it, so we cut the song.

The organization invited me to Washington, D.C. to perform the song for the 10th anniversary celebration on the steps of the Nation's Capitol. They flew me up there and, of course, I took Tim along. As he sat on the steps and I was up there singing and looking out over the monuments, I felt my life had been so miraculously protected and God had done so much for me even though I had struggled through so much. I saw my beautiful, intelligent, loving son sitting there on the steps of the Nation's Capitol. I was in a white silk dress with the wind blowing through my hair while all these Congressmen, Senators and thousands of others celebrated this incredible occasion. All I could do was say, "Thank you, God that you let me experience this and come full circle from that little club down the road."

Tim was no longer in a little playpen with a baby bottle in his mouth upstairs in that beer joint while I performed downstairs. He was now this young handsome college student attending Vanderbilt University. How far we had come through faith! God has always given me the courage to go on and to move on in spite of the struggles in my life.

I do a lot of work with domestic violence organizations, women and children's shelters, and similar projects. It's an important cause because rape, sexual abuse and domestic violence are prevalent problems in our society. Some don't like to talk about it. Many politicians and celebrities shy away from it. Everybody loves to get in on a popular issue but this is not a popular topic. We need to confront the issues that need to be confronted and be courageous enough to stand up and speak out.

I asked a friend of mine to sing a song with me for a television show. The show was about domestic violence. She paused and then she almost scolded me saying, "Stella, I'll sing it with you, but don't you expect me to talk about my family's situation."

Many people used to criticize Mother's Against Drunk Drivers, but they do so much good. Because of their efforts, the drunk driving law is now in place. It was the most incredible experience hearing the stories of these individuals. I met so many victims who had been burned and disfigured in alcohol-related accidents because of the irresponsibility of others. People don't like to hear about it but we all know it's on the news everyday.

I often think we don't need to worry about terrorists blowing us off the planet. We are destroying ourselves through drug and alcohol abuse, ruining the lives of our children. This is supposed to be the greatest country in the world and it is. We do indeed have so much freedom, but our children and helpless mothers are being held hostage every day living with the real terrorists in their own homes. Only God can help us.

Anyway, I was grateful to have the opportunity to serve as a spokesperson for this wonderful organization. Through their efforts, we now have all these public service spots on television, running one right after another, especially during the holiday season. Those public service announcements urge putting car keys in the hands of designated drivers. The idea has finally become popular, but back when the campaign started, it was not popular at all.

Domestic violence prevention, also, is not an in-vogue cause, and many don't want to hear about it. Many of us have been victimized by domestic violence, a rape, or abuse of some kind. And we're all acquainted with someone who has had that experience.

One of my closest cousins I've known since I was five and she was four moved to Washington to take care of Tim while I was working. She was like a surrogate mother to him in my absence. What a miracle to have a relative live with us who helped take care of my baby. It was a blessing because I was a struggling entertainer and not well off financially. When Tim turned nine and went to military school, she moved out and no longer lived with us.

After she moved away, she met and married a man and moved to Chicago. I believed she was happy. We would talk occasionally and they came to visit a time or two. Although he was much older, I never thought much about it. She was working as a cook in a restaurant and they were having what I thought was a good life.

Then one day I was on the road doing a play, and I got a call that she was in a hospital in Chicago and I should call her immediately. She was in the hospital because of a beating. She was there for several weeks. After being released, she stayed in a women's shelter for quite some time since she was unable to care for herself because of the severity of the beating. She was still living in the shelter when the tour took me through Chicago several weeks later.

Two of the women from the shelter brought her over to see me at the theater. They came backstage to my dressing room before the show started. I already had eyelashes on and all my stage makeup applied. Then I saw my precious, sweet friend who had helped me raise my baby. I didn't recognize her. It was the hardest thing for me to see one of my best friends in the whole world in such terrible shape, and to see how she was so helpless. To this day, it brings tears to my eyes when I remember how she looked.

One night she had come home from work, so tired after working hard all day, and her husband was drunk. He somehow had it in his mind that she was having an affair. Of course, she hadn't – it was all in his mind. His drunken state had convinced him of it.

"Oh, you're drunk," she told him, then walked into the bedroom and got undressed to take a shower. After she got into the shower, in a rage he came in and pulled her out by the hair of the head. He dragged her out of the bathroom and beat her into a pulp. She tried to fight him off, she said. She was no match for him. She's a little woman, about my size. And he was a big, tough steelworker.

He threw one of his denim shirts at her, made her put it on, then he marched her down to the parking area of the apartment complex where they lived. This is in the middle of Chicago's winter. He shoved her into the trunk of the car and drove to the city dump where he planned to finish her off.

I asked her what she was doing and thinking during this awful time.

"I was praying," she told me. "I was mostly praying Momma and Daddy wouldn't have to know I died this way. They wouldn't have to know I had been beaten to death and thrown into the garbage dump."

That would have been a horrible fact to face for her kind and gentle Christian parents. This is why I believe that God does protect us. Unfortunately, not everyone gets away.

She was praying while she was in the dark trunk half-naked and freezing. "God, just let me stay alive until he passes out," she prayed. "Don't let Mommy and Daddy find out I died this way."

Suddenly, she felt the car turn around and change directions. Soon she felt the car go over speed bumps. She knew those were the speed bumps in the parking lot of her apartment building. He got out of the car, opened the trunk and dragged her back upstairs and into the apartment, beating her still. This went on for several more hours. She kept praying to stay alive until he passed out and she could escape.

Finally, he did pass out and she crawled out the door and down the hall, wearing only the bloody shirt. Residents across the hall saw her and called the police and ambulance. They came and rushed her to the hospital. The police arrested him.

When I heard this story and looked at her disfigured face, I vowed to do everything I could to help women in domestic violence situations. It's a miracle she escaped from the horrible death he had planned for her. She suffered damage on her face and body, and spent months recovering. Yet, she has not allowed the vicious assault to damage her life. She refused to press charges because he was her husband. Wisely, though, she soon divorced him and never went back.

Now we're sleeping with the enemy
We're ready to give up
Sleeping with the enemy
What we've lost is trust
Yes, we're sleeping with the enemy
And it hurts so much
Sleeping with the enemy and the enemy is us

"Sleeping With The Enemy"
Written by: Stella Parton
©1995 My Mama's Music (BMI)

Just because you've been a victim of a rape or a domestic violence situation, or even years of abuse, doesn't mean you have to let it cripple your life. Now my friend lives in Nashville again. We usually spend New Year's Day together, just like always. She goes to East Tennessee to visit her family through the Christmas holidays, so our Christmas together is New Year's Day. We share black-eyed peas, cornbread, fried potatoes and turnip greens just like home. We always thank God for another year to be together.

She has a good job and has totally rehabilitated her life. This beautiful woman has never married again, and has no children, but she has a wonderful life. This demonstrates no matter what you go through, as long as you have life, the will to put things behind you and the will to move forward, you can.

Having dinner with a group of people not long ago, the subject of one of my many projects with the battered women's shelters came up. A man at the table said that women like men who abuse them. The entire table became quiet until I gave him my opposite views. I looked at his wife. She had her head down. Later in the ladies room she said, "Stella, I'm glad you spoke up." I said, "I'll start praying for you." Recently, he left her for a younger woman. I guess I need to start praying harder, but God performed a miracle in her life.

Another girlfriend of mine worked for a well-known country singer, and she was raped out on tour. One night she heard a knock on her motel door and thought it was one of the other girls in the band. She went to the door and didn't even look out because she thought it was someone she knew. Suddenly a stranger burst into her room and raped her. But she's not allowed it to cripple her. Instead, she has gone to therapy and become very involved in her rehabilitation from this trauma. She is now out helping others by using this experience in a positive way. But just like the man at dinner the other night, there will always be people who think we brought it on ourselves.

We can't always know how another person is going to process something, so we can't judge. I'm just speaking from my own experiences.

When I was 24 years old, I was invited to the stage of the Grand Ole Opry at the Ryman Auditorium. There was a reception for state legislators who were in session in Nashville. They had invited country music performers to join them. I wasn't really well known, but I was invited through my booking agency.

A couple of well-known, prestigious and successful politician-businessmen from my hometown attended the reception. Someone introduced me to them and they were friendly. I stayed about half an hour until I had to go home since my cousin needed to go to work at her other job. One of the men, now deceased, asked me if I'd drop off one of the legislators at his hotel. He was about the same age as my Dad. I had heard of him, but had never met him personally.

I didn't mind – it was just up the street from the Ryman. I drove him there and pulled under the canopy at the front door. He looked in the lobby and said, "Stella, if you wouldn't mind, would you drive me down to the basement parking lot. There are some folks in the lobby I have to meet but I need to run up to my room first to get some papers."

I drove down into the basement so he could take the elevator straight up to his room. After I put the car in park so he could jump out, I thought he'd say, "Thanks for the ride. It was nice meeting you Stella."

But, out of nowhere, he proceeded to attack me and pull me across the seat of the car. As he viciously assaulted me, tearing my clothes, I tried to fight him off. He cut my lip and blood began to squirt everywhere. I knew I was in deep trouble. For some reason, the only thing I could think of was to scream, "I'll tell my daddy!"

I figured he knew my dad because we had shopped at his establishment.

Yet when I yelled, he somehow came to his senses for a moment. Then he slapped me so hard he broke my nose. You can still see the scar on my face today where the bone popped through my flesh. He called me a bitch and shoved me across the car before he jumped out and slammed the door. This is a man I had given a ride to, and a person I knew from my hometown, and here I was fighting for my life.

When I got home, Darlene was there, and asked, "What in the world happened to you, Stella?"

"Well, I had to fight this man off." I told her and she said, "Who was it?" I told her. She said, "You're kidding! What are you going to do about it?"

I said, "What *can* I do? Nobody would believe he would do such a thing to me because of who he is." So I never told anyone.

Years later, I was home in Pigeon Forge, Tennessee, having a meeting with two businessmen who wanted to talk to me about opening a business. This man walked by the window of the office where we were meeting. They motioned for him to come in. This feeble old man shuffled in. Obviously, he was quite afflicted with some bad condition. One of them said, "I bet you don't know who this is, do you?"

He said, "I know *exactly* who she is," then looked right at me. "The last time I saw you was in Nashville."

I had a sick feeling when I realized this old man was the same one who had so violently attacked me many years before. "You're right," I said, "that's exactly where it was."

He was not repentant at all. It was as if he wanted to remind me of that horrible night.

The chance meeting with my attacker threw me into a deep depression for several months. Since then, I've been telling this story, mainly because you can't allow things of this sort to hold you back.

One day during this period, I was reading our local paper and saw where his daughter, who was my age, had died of cancer. It suddenly occurred to me that when I had screamed, "I'll tell my daddy!" he must have realized it could be his own daughter someone was attacking. Again, God protected me. I don't know what made me scream, "I'll tell my daddy", but it turned out to be, maybe, the only thing that saved me that night. Even though he backhanded me, broke my nose, ripped my clothes and called me a bitch, something brought him to his senses. I didn't know then if he had children or not. It never occurred to me because I had tried to put it out of my mind.

When I read about his daughter, I understood how God had saved me through the miracle of giving me exactly the right thing to say. Again, I was saved miraculously. No one would have thought that this prominent politician would have done such a thing, but he could have killed me. I could have ended up dying in the corner of the basement parking lot at that stupid hotel, and no one would have known what happened to me.

Because I didn't press charges, it looked as though he got away with his assault just like my friend's husband.

I can truthfully say I have never kissed a man without his asking me to. So why is it that some people think it's all right to say, "Well, she asked for it?" What a stupid load of crap that is! It's the same lame excuse as, "Well, I was drunk. I can't be held responsible for my actions." I don't buy that one either. Stupid people should not be allowed to drink, drive or have a wife and children to mistreat. I say get a life and stay away from mine. I really feel there should never be more than one chance on issues like this.

Other women should know they are not alone if something like this happens to them. Any face you look into probably has suffered horrible things no matter how happy or successful they appear. Don't be envious or jealous of someone, thinking they've got it made. Just know you are not alone, you can overcome it. As long as you're up and your brain is working, you can overcome.

We have choices we have to make. A happy life is one of those choices. Don't look for the curse - look for the blessing. Many people have told me, "If I were you, Stella, I wouldn't even try to have a career in music, trying to live in Dolly's shadow."

Isn't that the silliest thing? Isn't that the most defeatist attitude you've ever heard? Either I can allow it to be a curse or I can find the blessing in it. Yes, doors have been slammed in my face and there are those who resent me today because they think, "How *dare* she try to have a career with Dolly being so successful – I bet she gets hand-outs all the time, and I bet Dolly has done everything for her."

A few years ago, I was backstage at the Opry. There were several of us standing around talking. Another female singer was talking to me. She was telling me how bad things had been for her. She went on to tell me how angry she was for not being able to do more with her music. I said, "Well, why don't you just leave it in God's hands? I know He will work it out for you. I'll pray with you about it." She seethed at me with so much venom in her voice and said, "How would you know anything about what I'm going through. I'm sure Dolly has helped you every step of the way." Actually, I was very hurt and stunned. I was trying to reach out to her and offer her a word of comfort.

People don't really know my story. If you really knew, you'd be surprised not jealous. There are so many awkward situations to maneuver because of my relationship with my sister. People often think I should be able to cut right through the line and move on up to the front because Dolly has been at the top of her game so long. Then there are those who think I should not have tried to have a career in the same business. At times, I have thought they were right. But either I can look at it as a burden or I can look at it as a blessing. And I choose to look at it as a blessing. I don't know anyone who shouldn't be proud to be related to a person as talented as my sister, Dolly. I didn't have to buy it; I've been her sister since the day I was born. I don't have any excuses or apologies to make. It's my birthright and I didn't even marry into it.

I know an individual in Nashville who has very successful and well-known parents. This person has had a lot of opportunity, but has allowed their success to be crippling. Being in and out of the Betty Ford Clinic all the time, I said, "Are you addicted to the clinic?" They said, "I'm just afraid to try." I said, "What a cop out. Afraid to try to be a success? Get up and get over it."

Me, I'm a proud Appalachian woman and I dance to my own drum. I have my own life to live. It's my breath I'm breathing every day, not someone else's. God breathed the breath of life into me for a purpose. I don't fully know what my purpose is, but I know part of it is to do good whether it's in a small way or a monumental way. It's my choice to be positive and not blame others for my unhappiness.

If I'm unhappy about something, then I'd better be looking inside myself to find out why.

"Humans are divided into two parts: body and spirit. The body is like a house, but the spirit is like an automobile – always on the move."

– Flannery O'Conner

My Australian Blues Cure

In 1995, before one of my tours to Australia, I had been training with weights. My weights were so heavy I decided not to take them all the way to Australia. I decided I would just walk and try to keep up with my exercise program.

I was going through a lot of stress at the time, hurt over a betrayal. During the tour, I walked on the beach in Sydney every morning. As I inhaled the sweet air and enjoyed the water, sand and sun, I decided Australia was a magnificent place to visit, but too far away from my Appalachian Mountains.

One morning about 8 o'clock while walking on the beach, I was crying over the situation that had really hurt me. During the tour, I would well up and cry on my walk every morning. I was feeling so sorry for myself. I think it's all right to cry and grieve over hurt, but not to dwell on it. It's like a burning house. Get in and get out of it as soon as you can. But go ahead and go with your feelings. I was having a lot of trouble following my own advice.

I had been crying every day for a week. This particular morning I walked just as hard as I could. I started beating myself up for not being very athletic. I thought I should be able to run since I didn't have the weights. I've found that weight walking is my best exercise. Anyway, I was criticizing myself because I couldn't run. But I did have moments of being thankful. I was happy to be walking on such a beautiful beach. It was lined with magnificent trees on the bluff of Sydney Harbor.

While I was feeling so sorry for my pitiful behavior and inadequate physical ability to be a runner, a man came running past me. I didn't notice anything unusual.

Suddenly there were two more men behind him, quickly passing me. I looked up ahead and saw the man in front was running on an artificial leg. The other two must have been his trainers. Or else, he was their coach. I couldn't really tell.

It was the most sobering thing to see. I thought, how dare I criticize myself and not be thankful for the two legs I have. I may be walking but there's a man out there with one leg outdoing all of us on two legs.

Who am I to be criticizing myself and being ungrateful? What a slap in the face that was for me! I may have short legs, but I still have two.

The man running on the beach in the land Down Under showed me how to get up and get over it. *"The Lord preserveth the simple: I was brought low, and he helped me."* – *Psalm 116*

"There is nothing we cannot live down, rise above and overcome."

– Ella Wheeler-Wilcox

Saying No To "Oui"

When I was just beginning to hit the charts with my first records, in the late seventies, I got an offer to do a photo session for *Oui* Magazine.

I was in my twenties and still pretty naïve. For one thing, I had no idea what kind of publication *Oui* was. I thought it was like *People* or *Us*. There was *Time* and *Newsweek*, and I figured *Oui* and *Us* were the same type of periodical. I didn't know French or its pronunciation, so I thought it was "*We*". *We* and *Us* - pronouns. It made a lot of sense to me. Just another family magazine.

Oh, I got so excited when my publicist told me that *Oui* wanted to do a cover on me. I said, "Oh, great!"

I arrived at the photo session in Los Angeles and walked into the makeup room not suspecting a thing. I said, good morning to the hairdresser, and she pointed me to a corner, saying, "Your wardrobe is right over there."

I was looking for a rack of clothes, and there wasn't one. I walked over to the sofa where they had draped some red and black silk crotch-less panties and some lacy corset things that looked as though they were exhibits from an adult bookstore raid. "Where are my clothes?" I asked.

"What clothes?" they answered.

"This is underwear!" I'm so countrified I didn't even call it lingerie.

"Darn, it looks like the rats already got hold of these little frilly panties! The crotch is missing in every last pair!" They didn't even chuckle at my nervous little joke.

We had a lot to learn about each other.

By the time I got dressed in some clothes more suitable to me and they styled my hair, and applied makeup, I had already gotten into a fight with the photographer. He was a world famous photographer who had shot nude layouts for *Playboy, Penthouse,* and *Oui* and other magazines of the sort. He was what folks in the mountains would call a porno-grapher.

The photographer was upset because I wouldn't get naked for his little camera. I refused to wear those things that they had laid out for me. I did wear some little lacy anklets and a pair of tight satin shorts, and a little pink tank top. I felt like I was in an illegal abortion clinic for the seven hours I was there. I really did. I didn't want to disappoint my mom and dad and break their hearts. It was never a question for me because of my modesty. I would never have done anything to embarrass my family and least of all myself.

When I saw all the food, champagne and other mind altering "delights" they offered, coupled with them telling me how gorgeous I was, I could see why some of those girls stripped for their cameras. I must admit, though, the pictures turned out beautiful, and I am proud of them. I lost the cover of *Oui* because another well-known singer at the time took off more than I did. She got the cover for doing so. She showed her bottom and her breasts. I am so happy she won and I lost. Where is she these days? I don't think the extra exposure – pun intended – helped her career any. I am reminded of Proverbs 11:22, which says: *"A beautiful woman lacking discretion and modesty is like a fine gold ring in a pig's snout."*

If I had been into drugs and alcohol, and not brought up with strong convictions about right and wrong, who knows what I might have done? They were telling me how beautiful I was and how I should share my beauty with the world. Then there was the champagne and other entice-ments to sway me to such a decision. But little naïve, *East Tennessee Me* was so modest I hid even when I changed clothes because I was afraid they had two-way mirrors in the dressing room.

The photographer, in his frustration asked me, "Who do you think you are? What is it with all you country women from the South, thinking you've got 'something special' when it comes to sex?"

By then, I was getting pretty frustrated and angry myself. And I said, "Let me tell you something, buddy! I have a dad and five brothers at home. And there's no way I can go home if I got naked and those pictures showed up in your magazine." Of course, I threw in a few choice cuss words for effect.

Just before the shoot, my Hollywood managers came prancing in wearing their little Gucci loafers with the tas-sels on the top and carrying their little shoulder purses. I jumped down out of the make-up chair, ran over and started explaining the situation in my animated way. I just knew they would straighten this guy out, but they looked at each other like the Keystone Cops and said, "Well Stella, it's not that big a deal. It might also help us sell a few records." I was caught between a rock and a hard place.

The photographer shook his head angrily, but gained some understanding about the potential consequences of the situation when I went on to say, "You wouldn't want to deal with the men in my family if they happened to see nude photos of me in this stupid magazine. They are all as mean as those guys in that movie *Deliverance*. You don't want them over here after you. Do you? You know what I mean?"

He kind of grimaced and didn't have anything else to say to me after that little explanation. And neither did I after saying Yes, and No, to *Oui*, all in the same day.

Obviously, I had never seen *Deliverance* or I wouldn't have said that about my dad and brothers. Later, when I was back home telling my family about it, one of my brothers yelled at me for saying such a thing. He must have seen the movie.

Oh, well, I told you I was naïve.

"Tis easy enough to be pleasant when life flows along like a song, but the one worthwhile is the one who will smile, when everything goes dead wrong."

– Ella Wheeler-Wilcox

Touring Musicals And Snarling Dogs

I have been fortunate to have had the opportunity to play the leading role in several theatrical productions, some of them touring musicals with companies out of New York.

I learn a lot in these productions and really enjoy this type of performing because it involves singing, dancing and acting. A show of this sort depends on each person in the cast to present it properly. It's not the same as a concert where the band is onstage to support you.

One of the shows I toured with back in the early eighties was *The Best Little Whorehouse In Texas*. It was a good production, we had a nice cast for the most part, and some very fine young dancers. For some of these kids, it was their first experience away from home. Most of them were barely out of their teens and some were just out of high school.

We had been on tour for a month or so when I noticed the spotlights had changed. During my time onstage for several nights, the spotlight was always focusing in on me when it shouldn't have been. The blocking had not been changed but I just let it pass, assuming someone new was running the lights and they would get it worked out.

One night during this time, we had a cast party at one of the hotels where we were staying. We were going to be performing in Spokane, Washington for a few days, which wasn't typical. Usually, we did only one show in each town and we left for the next town right after the show each night. We would drive to the next city and arrive in the early morning hours just in time for me to check in, shower and go to the local TV station for a noon show appearance and do radio and newspaper interviews. It was not very glamorous. And I have always needed my rest. (As the Donna Summer song goes, *"she works hard for the money."*)

Anyway, that night after the party some of us got on the elevator to go to our rooms. Mostly the girls but a few guys got on as well. One of the men in the stage crew offered to carry my guitar and I said okay. When we got to my room, I opened the door and walked in to place my purse on the dresser and take off my coat and hang it up. I just naturally assumed he would put my guitar down and I would say thanks and good night before closing my door for the evening.

As I turned around, he had closed the door behind him and was glaring at me with a strange look on his face, almost like that of a snarling dog. I glanced at my guitar propped against the wall. Suddenly, before I could think straight, he quickly stepped toward me, shoved me on the bed, and was on top of me. Somehow, I came to my senses and realized what was going on.

I began to smile and act as though I was going along with him. I whispered I needed to go to the restroom first and moved out from under him. I was still fully dressed. Still smiling I tiptoed in the direction of the restroom and the door. I flung the door to my room open and stood in the hall yelling at the top of my lungs for him to get out of my room. I started to knock on every door I could reach as he came out in the hall. Some of the other people started unlocking their doors and were coming out to see what was going on.

While he was denying my accusations, in the confusion, I managed to get back into my room somehow and lock the door. I could barely dial the phone from shaking so violently. I screamed in the phone for security to come right away as he yelled and continued to beat on my locked door.

Once they had him downstairs and security called the police, the company manager called my room for an explanation. After all his denials and my demands to get him off the show, the company manager pleaded with me not to press charges because it would ruin the tour for the entire cast. I didn't press charges because of the publicity and the concern for the show and the cast.

A few days later, some of those young girls in the show came forward after he was long gone. He had taken advantage of at least three of them. That's when I learned that he was the spotlight operator. They were too afraid to come forward. I tell this story just to show how much damage can occur if we are afraid to speak out.

Once again, I was protected and I consider it a miracle it turned out as well as it did.

Another thing happened on that same tour. I enjoy telling this story because it is so funny. I don't want you to be shocked and think I only tell the negative stuff.

Anyway, three months into the six-month tour, the cast bus started having mechanical problems. The bus had about twenty-eight people on it, and each person had one seat to sit, sleep and live in on the road for six months. How glamorous! Ain't show biz grand?

I had my own bus, with kitchen facilities, which made it easier for me. Although I did have to get to the next city each day before everyone else and cover all the publicity while they could sleep until show time. I had no name on my bus because I am somewhat shy about being too showy somehow. Especially after being parked in the Wal-mart parking lot one day and gathering a crowd.

I started out with the "*Whorehouse*" logo on my bus, too, but had it taken off after a couple of days. I was standing in the kitchen area with my head wrapped in a towel and a bathrobe on. I was frying potatoes, making myself a good ol' country meal. I was totally oblivious to everything going on around me when suddenly I looked out the window and saw about a half dozen people jumping up trying to get a good look at me. I was startled and embarrassed to see that many strangers looking at me while I looked so tacky. I wasn't sure if they might have mistaken my bus for a brothel on wheels. The bus driver was a little bit disappointed when I made him remove the logo. I think he was enjoying all the attention at my expense.

The cast bus kept their logo and got lots of whistles and horns blowing. It gave us a lot of attention as we rolled from town to town. One Sunday morning their bus broke down directly in front of a big Baptist Church, rolling to a complete stop in the parking lot. I'm giggling even now wondering what in the world the members of the church thought as they pulled into the parking lot that Sunday morning and what in the world the pastor must have preached on that day. I consider it a miracle I was not on that bus because I would have died from embarrassment. I must have been living right that week.

In this production, as in most of the work I have done throughout my career, I have met many homosexuals. I know what homosexuality is, but not why it is. What I do know about it is that many people are in a real state of ignorance about it. Theories abound, though, everything from nature to nurture, or some blending of the two.

Those who discover their homosexuality at an early age carry a great burden. Today's Christian faith generally views homosexuality as an abomination and getting Christians to discuss the matter raises great anxiety. For instance, I asked a minister whom I hold in great respect to read this section, and he said, "Stella, I wouldn't put this in your book." He felt that it was not something I should bring up because too many Christians would be very upset with me for having homosexual friends. This man is the most knowledgeable Bible scholar I know and he wouldn't even discuss it.

Jesus taught compassion. He did not teach us to judge others. Jesus said he came not to judge because God is the judge.

Most homosexuals I know feel it is a curse on their lives. Living this way is awkward for most of them because their families and communities judge and look down on them. Perhaps we should search our hearts about…the *hardness* of our own hearts.

Are any of us righteous enough to justify cruelty to others because of our individual prejudices? Over the years, I have become very good friends with some individuals who are homosexual. One of my friends died of AIDS a few years ago and I was able to comfort him through the ordeal of this dreadful disease. In the last few weeks of his life, he accepted salvation. God let me be there for him to pray the prayer of faith. What if I had shunned him, judged him or withheld my love and respect from him? Would I not be judged for my *hardness* of heart? I remember our friendship fondly.

One of my dearest friends, who happens to be a homosexual, is one of the kindest, most generous human beings I know. To my knowledge, he has had only one relationship in his adult life, yet he has carried this burden and kept his family uninformed about it. My dear friend has provided and cared for his parents and sibling and helped to raise a niece and nephew. I have watched him spend all his earnings on their care and education. This man is one of the kindest, most caring human beings I know. Should I hesitate to call him a friend?

I am not wise enough to understand certain aspects of humanity, but I pray that rather than understanding that I can love my fellow man.

A year or so ago an old friend of mine suddenly lost her husband to a heart attack. The funeral service occurred in a funeral home down the street. My friend asked a retired Catholic priest at her church to conduct the service and he agreed. He showed up wearing a brown tweed jacket with suede patches on the elbows and a flannel shirt underneath. His casual attire struck me as odd.

He carried a yellow legal pad and read a few vital statistics on my friend's life, since he was not personally acquainted. The priest invited others to come up and speak. I took my place at the podium. The priest sat in a chair a couple of rows back on the aisle. I shared a few things about my friendship with this loving couple over the years and asked if I could read a short verse from the scripture that seemed appropriate. My friend nodded yes. As I read, I noticed the priest had his head in his hands. I thought, "Oh my, the poor man must have a headache or something." Quickly, I finished the five or six lines of scripture and told my friend I loved her and would be praying for her peace and comfort during this time.

I returned to my seat and the priest got up, thanked everyone for coming, and concluded the service without a prayer. We began to get up from our chairs and said our goodbyes when I saw the priest coming toward me with an angry look on his face. He was flushed and angry. I thought, "Goodness, I wonder why he is so upset?" I found out immediately. He admonished me for reading from the Bible and told me I had most definitely offended the non-Christians in attendance. I was shocked, and so were several people standing around. They were saying how nice my talk had been. A couple of the women actually put their hands to their chests and faces in shock at his anger toward me. Just as quickly, he wheeled around and was gone.

Stunned, the ladies asked me if I was okay. Although in disbelief, I assured them that I was fine and that we should be quiet so my friend would not hear what had occurred.

We were all there to show our love and support. What was his problem?

I wonder how many innocent children's lives have been altered or destroyed by sick and twisted authority figures in their young lives. I wonder how many women have sought out the advice of an authority figure like this priest and have been belittled or given bad advice. I know I have experienced this type of treatment more than once in my life.

A few days later, my friend called to thank me for coming to speak at her husband's memorial service. She went on to say another friend told her of the priest's treatment. She apologized. I told her not to worry about it. Then she said, "Well Stella, if it's any consolation, poor Father Maloney locked himself out of his car that night and had to wait for over three hours in the freezing cold for a locksmith to come and open his car!" I told my son about the incident and he said, "That could be considered instant karma, Mom."

I believe in a loving God. The scripture says God is love. I felt bad for the poor priest standing somewhere all alone in the cold February night air wearing just a tweed jacket. Maybe his habit would have been warm in that situation.

Bottom line is we never really know another person's reality. That is why we should never judge another. God, have mercy on us all.

In the early seventies, I was booked for a nightclub performance in Texas and I flew there from Nashville, Tennessee. I had thrown my back out and could hardly walk, but I needed the money because I had just moved so I was still out on the road working. The nightclub owner was very hateful and mean when he met me at the airport. After driving me to the motel where he had booked me a room, he carried my bag upstairs since I was walking on a cane.

"Thank you, I appreciate it," I told him. "You can have somebody come back in an hour and pick me up and take me to the club."

"No," he said, "you can change clothes right now." He said, "I'm not leaving." That's when I realized he was expecting more than a singing performance from me, because he refused to leave my room. I was in a panic. There I was alone with a stranger in the middle of Texas, wondering what in the world I would do. Terror doesn't adequately describe my feelings at that moment.

He apparently thought that because he paid me to come and sing and that since I was a performer, it was not out of the question to have me perform in a different way in that shabby motel. I'd heard stories. Some people assume entertainers have loose behavior, but that is not true. We are no different from other people. I know people in other professions who behave worse than most entertainers I know. The only difference is, we end up in the news if we do anything at all.

Anyway, I used what wits I had at that moment. I chose not to change into my stage clothes while he was leering at me. Going into the bathroom to change was out of the question because I would be backed into a corner.

"I'll just go like this," I blurted out. And I went in the wrinkled clothes I had worn all day while traveling. You have to be fast on your feet sometimes – and I've had to do that sometimes more than I've wanted. It's called survival, and I've had numerous situations of this sort. He bullied me from the start, so I knew I was in trouble – and the night was just beginning. So I started praying as soon as I sat down at the table near the stage before the show. I prayed, "Please, God, send somebody to help me, please."

Out of the blue, a waitress came to my table and said, "Stella, there's a man over at the bar who wants to know if you got your roses."

"Roses?"

"Yeah. Roses."

"No. But who sent me roses? Who is he?"

"He said he went to high school with you," she said.

"Well, tell him to come over."

She told him what I had said. He walked over to my table and sat down. What a relief to see him! His name was Bobby, I had gone to high school with him, and we had been good friends. I quickly told him, "Oh, you *have* to sit here. Thank God you're here!"

"Goodness, what are you doing in this place?" Bobby asked me with a worried expression on his face.

Embarrassed I said, "I'm making a living – what do you think I'm doing?"

"You don't need to be in this place by yourself. I told my wife I was coming down to say hi to you."

"Why didn't she come with you?" I asked.

"I wouldn't want her in a place like this. Stella, this is the roughest place in the area."

"Well, call her and tell her you're going to have to stay here all night because you have to get me to the airport."

When I told him where I was staying, he said, "You can't stay there – that's a hooker hotel!"

It was a miracle he was there for me, just coming out of nowhere when I desperately needed him for my safety. At a time when I had no one else to turn to, God sent someone. Bobby told me he had been sitting home and decided at the last minute that he would come down and see me. He had sent me roses that never came or that someone had taken.

"I'll phone her," he said.

"Okay, tell her I'd really appreciate it if you could do this for me."

"I'm not going to let you down. I'm your friend."

Those are two miracles.

But that wasn't the end of my troubles with that lecherous nightclub owner. After the show, I had to meet with him in his office to be paid.

So Bobby said he would wait in the car and keep it running." "Go get your money if you can, and I'll drive you back to the airport to catch your plane in the morning." I always caught the earliest flight back home because I didn't want to be away from Tim longer than necessary.

After the owner realized I wasn't going to sleep with him, he didn't want to pay me for the show. He had avoided me all evening. It was wintertime and I wore a big overcoat, as I was getting ready to leave with my earth angel - Bobby. Hidden in my coat pocket was a little cassette tape recorder that I had turned on. I was really getting dramatic by this point because of the stress. I thought a recording of our conversation might be useful in a lawsuit if he didn't want to pay me.

I was a bit on guard because I had been stiffed on a job in Moline, Illinois the week before and had gotten home with exactly fifty-seven cents in my pocket. I was not about to let this happen to me again if I could help it.

The owner kept stalling as Bobby waited patiently outside for me. I really needed the money because my bills were due. This guy was going to make me stay until everybody else left, so that he could make his move again. Finally, everyone left except one other employee. I went into his office, and he was even more indignant because he now figured I had a boyfriend with me.

My fear of him started to mix with anger. I thought, "How *dare* you not pay me my money. You've worried the heck out of me, and now you don't even want to pay me? I don't think so!"

Finally, he just refused to pay me. I don't know what came over me, but here's how I handled it: I walked up to him with my hand in my trenchcoat pocket. I stuck the tape recorder into his side as if it was a gun. "I want my money, and I want it now!" I yelled, jamming the "concealed weapon" into his side just like a hit man would do it.

He was intoxicated and red in the face and started swearing at me. You should have heard the names he called me! I thought I knew how to cuss, but I picked up a couple of new words that night. He reluctantly gave me the money while cussing all the time, thinking I was going to shoot him if I didn't get it. What a miracle! A miracle that I made manifest.

As soon as the money was in my hand, I ran out of that building without even counting it and jumped into the waiting car with my walking cane in the air. We rushed over to the hotel and went upstairs to get my bag. My room door was open – it wasn't even locked. That's how unsafe the place was.

It didn't take me long to clear out of that room. I hadn't even opened my suitcase earlier because I had been afraid to change clothes with this man in my room.

My friend, Bobby, rescued me that night. Lord only knows what I might have had to deal with at the nightclub or at the No-tell Motel with a door that wouldn't even lock. But I knew enough to pray. That experience inspired this song:

> *But I'll hold you in my thoughts forever*
> *You will always be in my memory*
> *And I know I'll always remember*
> *The man that called me lady*

"The Man That Called Me Lady"
Written by: Stella Parton
©1981 My Mama's Music (BMI)

I think back on this incident today and wonder how I could have done such a thing.

My message here is don't ever underestimate the power of prayer or an angry Parton in a trenchcoat with a loaded tape recorder, bills to pay and a walking cane in her hand.

"So it always is. Someone is ever ready to scatter little acts of kindness along our pathway, making it smooth and pleasant."

– Helen Keller

Angels Along The Way

I lead an exciting life. Someone told me it would make an interesting movie…if people would only believe it.

Recently, I did a number of in-store promotions for the Ingles grocery store chain, signing autographs and selling my cookbooks. I wanted the tour to be a blessing to someone because the Ingles Corporation had partnered with me to promote their stores, sell my cookbooks and donate a portion of the proceeds to the battered women's shelters in each town I visited. And in every store I visited, God truly sent someone to whom I could witness.

During a stop in North Carolina, a young woman came in with a beautiful little girl who was about three years old. This child was flawless. She just took my breath away.

The mother sat the child in the buggy, but didn't stop at the autograph table because the line was long and she was in a hurry. After they went around the store and came back, the crowd had thinned a bit and she walked up to me. I said, "I have to tell you, you have the most beautiful little girl."

"Thank you," she said gently.

Suddenly, I realized the child was not reacting as a normal child should. I got up from the table, went over, touched her, and asked, "How are you?"

"I'm Stella Parton," I told the mother. "Your little daughter is just flawless."

"That's what my husband called her last night. Flawless," she said. "We are so proud of her, and she has just started to say a couple of words." Then she paused and said, "My baby is autistic."

I know some healing touch techniques that I demonstrated for her. I told her, "This is all for a reason. If you'll let God use you for a reason, and let her be the blessing God has brought her to be."

Now it was hard for me to say this because I have a perfectly healthy child, but at the same time, she needed hope and encouragement.

"You have no idea how hard this is," she told me.

"Oh, angel. There is no way I could know, but let me just give you a hug anyway and hold you." We stayed in a loving embrace for a long moment. I felt the pain and tension soften in her body.

That's all I could give her, but I did promise that I would pray for her and her little girl every day. And I do. Every time we go out, we need to be a blessing.

On another stop, a little woman came on the bus. She was about 75, and the spunkiest, cutest little woman, as full of spit and vinegar as she could be. She loved the tour bus and said, "Boy, I want this thing. I can get me a man, and he can take me across the country in this thing."

"This is Michael my driver," I said, pointing to the bus driver. She couldn't hear very well and thought I said, "This is Michael my lover."

"Your *lover*?"

No, my *driver*!"

Michael is a real shy little man and his face started turning red. But that didn't stop her.

"Your lover? I need this bus and I need your lover to drive me across country!"

She was so funny and so cute. We laughed and laughed. And Michael finally got over his embarrassment enough to start laughing, too.

She went on to do her grocery shopping, and I stood outside the door of the bus because it was a nice warm day and the perfect place to sign autographs and to visit with everyone. Later, after shopping, she came back around and started talking to me.

The more she talked, the more I realized she was an unconventional Christian like me. Unconventional, in that she was not your typical soft-spoken, church going, reverent woman. She told me about her daughter abandoning her 15-year-old terminally ill child. This spunky little woman is now taking care of her grandchild - this little woman, so full of spirit, so full of love, and so full of life. I stopped everything and said, "Well, let me pray with you."

Many people may think this is really outrageous or silly. It was an opportunity I could not let go by. I had to let her know she mattered and what she was doing was so important. She is definitely an earth angel and God had a great purpose in her living this long so that she could do this.

What a miracle for her that she is healthy enough to take care of this child. What a miracle for him that she loves him enough and is physically able to take care of him. And what a miracle for me to be reminded once again of my own blessings.

Miracles work in two ways. They are all about giving and receiving. You have to know how to receive your miracles. You have to know how to share the blessings as well as receive them.

I teach a 12-hour workshop titled *"Beauty on a Budget"* for underprivileged and abused women. It's about self-esteem and self-image. Most of the time they get the blessing I share in my class. Yet, there have been a few times that women are so angry and full of rage about what they've gone through that they literally avoid my touch. It's as if they hate everyone because of their anger. They're not ready for a blessing. Unless you're ready to receive your blessing, you won't get it. You must open up and trust in order to get it – it won't come through a wall of hate, mistrust or anger.

While driving down the road recently, I saw a man about my age thumbing a ride. The man looked disheveled and maybe like he was drunk. Each time a car passed him, there in broad daylight, where all the other traffic could see, he gave the old "hillbilly salute," throwing up his middle finger very angrily. I laughed as I drove past. Underneath my breath I said, "Yes sir, you're sure to get a ride that way." His anger prevented him from receiving the very thing he desired.

You've seen children throw a tantrum. You hand them a toy and they throw it back at you or you try to feed them a bite of food and they spit it on you. That's what we're doing when we don't allow ourselves to receive our blessings.

Miracles are there for the taking. It's up to us to let them in, nourish them, cherish them, and share them.

"What becomes of lost opportunities? Perhaps our guardian angel gathers them back up and will give them back when we've grown wiser – and will use them rightly."

– Helen Keller

Shadows & Stagelights

One of the most incredible blessings has been to see my life come full circle. I believe life is a wheel and we go around many times. I guess I'm probably on my third, fourth or fifth rotation.

I was a very reluctant entertainer and always thought I would be a missionary instead. When I was a little kid, I wanted to be a nun. I told my Mama and she asked, "Why do you want to be a nun?"

"Well, I want to marry Jesus." I had heard that's what nuns did, and I wanted to marry Jesus, too.

"Honey, you can't be a nun because we're not Catholic," she'd say.

Not that we didn't *look* like Catholics with 11 kids running around.

As soon as I accepted there was no way I could become a nun, I decided to become a missionary. I was reluctant to do anything except Christian work. Then in order to buy baby milk and support my family, I found myself working in clubs in the Washington, D.C. area. That was a very difficult time for me as a young woman, performing in a nightclub with Tim upstairs in a playpen. I'd go downstairs, do my shows, come back upstairs, feed him, diaper him, leave someone up there to watch him, and then go back down for another show.

I became a single mother when Tim was three and a half, and life was a struggle at times. I've gone through many different challenges.

A few years ago, one of my relatives asked, "Stella, why aren't you bitter after all the things you've been through?" I guess they were referring to my career struggles and broken marriages and having to raise Tim as a single mother. I didn't quite know how to answer for a moment. I thought about it and said, "Well, I don't have time to be angry or bitter. I have too many things to do. I am happy in spite of it all. Each disappointment, failure, betrayal and missed opportunity is a blessing because that is how I choose to regard it."

When I first started singing in Washington D.C. in December of 1969, I stepped into a different world. I was around politicians in Washington, Mafia types around Baltimore and various others in the clubs. It was sometimes frightening and it took strength to be in this world but not of it. During this time, my husband, Carroll, the father of my son, was always there. My manager and his wife were there to look after me, as well. One of my uncles came to work at the club for a while. After being there a few months, another uncle who lived in Nashville called for me to fly down for a meeting. He was working in the music publishing company for my sister, Dolly, and Porter Wagoner.

Carroll, Tim, my manager, Earl, and I flew down to see what was up. To my surprise, Porter and my sister, Dolly, were there for the meeting. After awkward greetings, my uncle proceeded to tell us that they had been discussing my working in Virginia. They had all decided it was necessary for me to stop singing immediately!

My uncle even pointed his finger at me across his desk. Tim was so young; he was still sitting on my lap sucking his bottle. I remember it as if it was yesterday. He said, "You need to take that kid of yours and go back home and work in the beauty shop where you belong."

Needless to say, I was struck numb and dumb all at once. My manager got a little hot under the collar hearing what was going down. After a few heated verbal exchanges between my uncle, Porter and my manager, Earl, Dolly quietly spoke up and said, "Well Stella, if you're going to sing you need to change your name."

I said, "What name?"

She said, "Well, how about Stella Mae?"

I said, "Okay, I guess I could if you'll start calling yourself Dolly Rebecca."

My uncle went on to say, they had decided it "might" hurt Dolly's career if I was "in the music business." The next day, heartbroken, I flew back to Washington. My manager was so angry with all of them. I was just hurt and confused. Carroll was sad and felt helpless, not knowing how to help me.

My manager promptly fired my other uncle after we returned. He then made me sit down and listen to taped telephone conversations he had been making of my two uncles discussing my shows every night. I listened as they discussed how big the crowds were, the response I was getting, the quality of my performance and all the things my manager was doing to promote me. I was stunned to hear them cook up a plot to get me back to Tennessee "where I belonged." I still find it hard to believe after all these years. As Dr. Phil would say, this was one of my defining moments.

People who were supposed to love me had gotten so caught up in such paranoia, ignorance and greed. My parents would have been devastated but they never knew. It's been difficult to see how both my sister and I were affected by this little game. As the years have gone by, I've seen how little it has benefited anyone.

Finally, I decided the best thing to do was to change my name to something else altogether. My married name at the time was German and very difficult to spell and pronounce. So we decided to go with Tim's middle name, which was the same as his dad's, Carroll, since it was easy to pronounce.

Some time later, I flew my parents up to Washington. It was a really big deal for me to be able to take them to see the White House and to give them an airplane ride and to go see President Kennedy's grave. I have such wonderful pictures of that trip. That was the only time my Daddy flew on a plane. During their visit, I told them I had decided to change my name. They were both very hurt. With tears in his eyes, my Dad said, "Stel, are you ashamed of your family now?" My Daddy was from the Appalachian Mountains and he had his own way of thinking.

I knew better than to tell him what had prompted my decision, because both my uncles and Porter would have been pleading for mercy from my Dad. Dolly and I might have found ourselves back home hoeing corn and tobacco. After that, I decided I'd just be who I am regardless of what anybody else thought. Out of respect for my sister, I always put a clause in my work contracts that her name cannot be used to promote my appearances.

However, I became terrified to see the anger my manager had for my family. I could not believe he had been taping all the phone conversations that were being made from the club where I worked. In the dark of night, Carroll and I left Virginia with what few things we had, making our escape while my manager was in the hospital recuperating from a car accident. Eventually, my manager forgave me for leaving, but he never managed me again.

Despite the family roadblocks, I've made it on my own, doing better than I ever dreamed possible. But that wasn't the only time others have tried to pit my sister and me against each other over the years. After all, I was barely twenty and she was just three and a half years older. We were both little girls who were pawns in the greedy little schemes of others. Not long ago, someone tried to make me feel bad over my sister and I suddenly spoke up in her defense and said, "Hey, if my sister was sick and needed me, I would take care of her. I believe she would *hire* someone to do the same for me. That's the way it is when you're family."

Some years ago when I owned a little café in Pigeon Forge a couple came in. They were seated at a table in the dining area. I was in the music room tuning my guitar and autoharp for the show that evening. The curtains were pulled and no one knew I was there. It was about 4:00 in the afternoon. The only customers at the time were this couple, and I could hear the conversation going on between the woman and the café manager.

She complained from the moment she came in - not about the service or the food but rather about my family. She went on and on making very rude comments about me. She knew I wouldn't be there, she said, probably wasn't any good anyway and the only reason I had my establishment was that Dolly had given me the money to play around there. What a joke that was! My sister did not have one dime of her money invested in my establishment.

This woman criticized other members of my family as well. Finally, she started to talk about Dolly and her weight problem and breast size. When she started on Dolly's plastic surgery, I could not stand it anymore. I put down my guitar and walked through the curtains and I introduced myself. She snidely looked at me, assessing my looks and my figure and made a negative remark about my weight. (Every woman knows that's a touchy subject.) She was hateful and rude. Finally I said, "Lady, you are the rudest person I have ever met and furthermore, at Dolly's highest weight she could fit into one leg of your pink polyester slacks. So if you don't mind, I'd appreciate it if you could find your way to the door and don't let it hit you in the backside as you leave." Of course, she was a little upset. As she snorted out the door, her poor little husband turned around, winked, smiled and said, "You young ladies have a good afternoon." He looked very happy that someone had finally stood up to her. Actually, I think he was afraid of her.

Not long after that, I chose to close my place because I got tired of that sort of thing because it happened almost daily. Anyway, I felt bad about telling her to leave. I had to pray for forgiveness for my temper yet one more time.

One day, not long after the incident, I was telling Tim I regretted having a temper and if I could just get a handle on that and a couple other things, I would be a better person. He smiled that little crooked grin just like my dad and said, "Mom, I'm glad you have a temper. What might have happened to us if you had not fought back at times?" Shocked I said, "Well, I am too opinionated." He said, "Well, you are the best Mom I've ever had." He bent down and patted me on the head, then laughed and walked out of the room.

I grew up feeling I wasn't supposed to be the way I am. For one reason or the other, I have always been apologetic for my behavior. Growing up with five older siblings who were critical of me, sometimes in very cruel ways, didn't help either. It's easy to see now that I've gotten older. Fortunately, I don't take things so personally anymore. However, I am a lot like my dad. I have my own way of thinking. It's just the mountain way.

People have always assumed that I relied on Dolly's help. I have always respected and loved my sister too much to take advantage of her. I see how some people with wealthy relatives take advantage. How must the successful family member feel knowing this? Most of my relatives aren't guilty of such behavior, although a few are less than blameless.

Truthfully, some relatives do take advantage, but it's not true of everyone in a family. Just because you're related to a celebrity doesn't automatically make you a freeloader. If anything, it has made it a lot more difficult in my situation. Of course, some family members will ask for money if they don't have any, for heaven's sake, but isn't that what families are for?

I have had friends, or people I thought were friends, who suddenly dropped me once I got them a job with my sister. One in particular was a friend for twenty years, or I should say I was her friend. Suddenly, I became a member of the *"boss'"* family and no longer a friend. I find it strange how she suddenly called me up, out of the blue, once she no longer worked for my sister, after ten years of hardly speaking to me.

This sort of treatment has been the most challenging for my family and me to handle. After all, we are just ordinary people dealing with being in the public eye. Most of my siblings feel uncomfortable with it, because it has been forced on them without their consent. I make it a point not to ask my family to participate in my career; after all, they have their own lives and they wouldn't dare ask me to do the same. If they need my help or support in any way, I always do what I can, as a sister but not as an entertainer.

Just because a family member becomes rich and famous doesn't make them right about everything either. It just makes them have more control. I think it's important not to abuse the position of power.

There are no books to teach a family how to deal with the sudden fame and fortune of a relative. Fame and fortune costs a family dearly, believe me. Just ask the families of O.J. Simpson, Michael Jackson and Bill Clinton. There has never been anything respectful said about the virtues of family members of celebrities. Comparisons begin and continue with the celebrity as soon as the relationship is made known. I knew Billy Carter and I felt very bad for him when his brother was in the White House.

When we came into the year 2000, I noticed many changes going on around me. My parents' health began to decline, and it saddened me to watch them getting so old and frail. I went through a very painful divorce. It was a very dark time for me in many ways. My Dad died the same week my divorce was final. My ex-husband didn't even send flowers to Dad's funeral. All I could do was pray for strength and guidance.

One day, I was praying "God, why is it that I can't seem to ever have a healthy relationship." Oh, I was crying, heartbroken and all torn down. Suddenly it was as if someone was in the room with me.

At that moment, I heard these words, "Stella, you are my bride and I am your bridegroom. Get in the 'Word.'" At that moment, I realized that if I were ever going to have a healthy relationship it would have to be with a man who also wanted to do some good with his life and to follow a spiritual path. We struggle enough in relationships without having differences in our spiritual lives. We cannot be unequally yoked as the Bible tells us. So I got back in the "Word" and began to study the scripture more diligently every day.

"That which was from the beginning, which we have heard, which we have seen with our eyes, which we have looked upon, and our hands have handled, of the Word of life." - John 1:1

I decided it was time for me to change everything about me that did not seem right. I felt I should use the name my parents had given me at birth - Stella. Yes, with a period at the end. So we designed a logo just this way. It appears on all my music these days. I don't hide the fact that I am Stella Parton – after all, I was given the name at birth by my parents. It belongs to me.

Actually, since the age of seven, I have been pulling my own weight. Since the age of 15, I have made my own way in life, never depending on anyone else to support me, neither my family nor the husbands I have had. I am blessed with good health and a healthy child. God let me sing my heart out and I believe music is the voice of God. I have been one of his little helpers spreading his goodness through song. How blessed have I been? Greatly blessed indeed.

A well-known singer once told me after seeing me perform on the Opry one night, "Stella, you are absolutely the most honest and sincere singer in the business."

I take that as a compliment. Mind you, he didn't say I was a good singer, but that's okay. Honest is good. Sincere is good. I credit God with protecting me through so many struggles. I always step forward and claim Jesus as my Saviour. Perfect I am not, yet I yearn most of all to tell the good news. The "good news" is the truth as I know it.

I belong to the family of God. In the sight of God, we are all his babies. I claim myself. I consider myself finally in my right mind and fortunate to have been born in America.

I believe in the Constitution of the United States and the Declaration of Independence, I thank all those who have sacrificed for this country. I believe in the Holy Bible and I believe Jesus is the Son of God and that He died on the cross for my salvation. I also believe that we should reach out to those less fortunate than ourselves with love, respect and acceptance. I believe we should treat animals, all of nature and our learning institutions in a sacred way. *"Trust in the Lord with all thine heart; and lean not unto thine own understanding. In all thy ways acknowledge him, and he shall direct thy paths." – Proverbs 3:5-6.*

I consider myself blessed to be a woman in this society. I am thankful for freedom of expression. It's amazing to note that even atheists who live in this country can complain about the word "God," in the Pledge of Allegiance and no one wants to have them arrested – well maybe a few people. As my daddy would say, "This country is free enough to let them outsmart themselves." I am most proud to be a mother. I consider myself a complete human being finally. I guess I've finally grown up.

I've given second chances to all of my friends
Forgiven my children and all of their kin
It's really no big deal, it happens all the time
It gets a lot easier time after time

I'll think about shadows another day
Shadows are always getting in my way
They're always with us come rain or come shine
I have decided to make friends of mine

When you get older you see it's all a game
You're in or you're out excuses can be lame
Who cares anyway, it's really no use
Just take your medicine, take it with juice

When I get to Heaven I know what I'll say
When asked about trouble along the way

I was being a blessing spreading good cheer
I won't have my shadows, they won't be there

I'll think about shadows another day
Shadows are always getting in my way
They're always with us come rain or come shine
I have decided to make friends of mine

"I'll Think About Shadows"
Written by: Stella Parton
©1995. My Mama's Music (BMI)

I'm sure I will get criticism for what I have written. I have lived long enough to know if you aren't doing anything, folks don't have any reason to talk about you. I share my experiences in the hope of being an inspiration to those who need to embrace their own individuality. We cannot think of ourselves as victims but as victors. I certainly don't mean to hurt anyone. However, everyone has a right to his or her dreams.

In the name of Jesus, we were all born for a purpose. No one else can fulfill our destiny. It is God's will that we all prosper and be in health. So laugh a little, love a lot and for goodness' sake be good for the sake of goodness and don't allow others to steal your joy or your birthright.

"Finally, it's honesty that heals."

– Suzanne Somers

Singin' For My Supper

In October 2004, I performed in Scandinavia. My appearance there was covered by the national news media and so I was on the radio, television, and the papers. On the early morning flight back home, some people recognized me. A young Nordic man with light red hair seated next to me asked for an autograph. He was hesitant at first but asked politely and apologized for bothering me. After all these years, I am still surprised when somebody acknowledges me as a "celebrity." Never knowing quite how to respond, I just try to put them at ease. In my own mind, I remain a little mountain girl sitting on the sled in the front yard with my big sister, Dolly, making up songs.

We would practice harmonizing and would make up lyrics together before I had even learned to write. One of my earliest memories is of her impatience with me because I couldn't come up with a satisfactory line in those early collaborations. I think I was always a pain in her neck. All I wanted was to be included in what she was doing. All she wanted was for me to get lost. The sibling rivalry started early I suppose, but I always saw it as her not liking me. It would be years before I realized she saw it as a competition.

This sibling rivalry, my mother's mental health issues dealing with depression, and my dad's alcohol problem have been my greatest hurts from childhood, not the poverty. I knew I needed love, nurturing, and respect. We all do. But how can you miss something you've never had? Later on in life, I became a perfect co-dependent, letting others walk all over me just trying to be loved and accepted.

Ironically, these things taught me patience, compassion and empathy. God gives us exactly what we need if we look within our hearts. Struggle has been a constant companion, but I have finally come to accept that a life without some struggle may be incomplete. Struggle, if seen through eyes of wisdom, builds character I believe.

From the beginning, music shaped my early memories of life. My sister, Cassie and I were sitting on the porch once, singing as we dangled our feet off the edge. We had made up a little song, and Daddy walked out and told us that we sounded so pretty he thought it was the radio. Now if that doesn't give a kid an ego boost, what would! He always encouraged our singing and showed so much pride when others complimented us.

Singing for family, friends and neighbors from early childhood, encouraged by Daddy and other relatives, was just a way of life for us. I was so young; in fact, I could not pronounce some words.

Daddy taught me to sing a funny song for visiting relatives. When I sang "Oh Do You Love Me Flossie Brown" everyone would roll with laughter because I sang…"Oh do my fossie fas you can." Once I realized they weren't laughing with praise, but because of my pronunciation, I ran away and hid, determined never to sing that song again. Only recently, have I discovered how typical of my Dad to find the humor in the innocence of my little song and how he was entertained by the antics of his children.

During those earlier years, Uncle Bill taught us harmonies and sometimes recruited Dolly, Cassie and me to sing backup on his rockabilly records. He still sells these recordings at "Dollywood." Now that I think of it, Daddy was right to laugh at us because we sounded like Alvin & the Chipmunks.

My Mom, sisters, and I sang at church services, funerals, family reunions, and school functions. My mother, Willadeene, Cassie and I recorded a gospel album entitled "In The Garden," when I was still a teenager. I listened to it just the other day and was surprised at how good the harmonies were.

After Dolly began working on the Cas Walker Show in Knoxville at the age of ten, she welcomed having the spotlight all to herself. It was wonderful for a kid who always had to take a backseat to seven younger siblings and fight to find her place with three older ones. Once she had experienced it, she guarded it fiercely and every time Mama said, "Dolly, you have to let Stel sing with you on TV the next time because you're always gone and she is having to do your chores and hers as well." Needless to say, she resented the notion of sharing and I suffered by being excluded.

Dolly found every reason in the world to keep me as far away as possible and over the years, I finally gave up and let her have it. However, I never stopped singing and writing songs. I competed in the Jr. Miss Pageant in high school, singing one of my own compositions. I didn't win, but I grew from the experience and later that year was voted most talented girl in my senior class. That was great validation and meant so much to me.

The first time I traveled to Nashville was on the bus with Dolly over a weekend when I was barely fourteen. She had a meeting with someone at Tree Publishing Company. Although Dolly was still in high school, she thought she was a "woman of the world." She had been in Nashville a few times already with Uncle Bill. I think Mama sent me along as some sort of protection figuring Dolly would be less likely to get into trouble if she had a kid sister tagging along. We argued the entire trip because of my chewing gum the whole time. This drove an already ticked off seventeen year old "woman of the world" a little mad.

We got off the bus and walked out on the street waiting for our cousin, Eva Young, to pick us up down on lower Broadway. We were staying at her house for the weekend. This being my first trip to the big city, I was wide-eyed to say the least. I looked across the street in the crisp, cold winter air and began gazing up at the height of the steeple on the First Baptist Church. Exclaiming to Dolly, "Gosh Dolly, look how tall that thing is." Looking just like Gomer Pyle, I'm sure. She gave me a swift elbow in the side and demanded, "Stop it because people will think we're from the country." I snapped back, "Well, we are from the country after all. I'm sure we've got 'em fooled." To this very day, I think about how funny we must have looked every time I drive past the First Baptist Church; Dolly in her big beehive hairdo and me looking like a tomboy tagging along.

Cassie traveled with me occasionally. Dolly once invited us to sing harmony with her at a Christmas party for the Salvation Army. Several Opry stars were there and were so complimentary, telling us we sounded as good as the Lennon Sisters and as good if not better than the Davis Sisters because of the blend of our voices. I remember Grandpa Jones telling us we should be a sister act like the Carter Family. Not long after that, Dolly got the opportunity to work with Porter Wagoner ending any dreams I fostered of being part of "the Parton Sisters."

Cassie always cried when we boarded the bus back to East Tennessee. I felt like crying myself, but Dolly and I would joke around with her until the bus pulled out, leaving Dolly standing alone waving goodbye to us as we pulled away. It still makes me sad when I think about it. We were still very attached to her and missed her terribly. Her letters home prompted Mama's efforts to send us down to be with her.

Throughout high school, I sang at every opportunity. Although I liked Elvis and the Beatles, my favorite music was the Motown sound; I also liked Chuck Berry, Fats Domino and Ray Charles. I loved the Supremes, seeing them as a black version of what I thought Dolly, Cassie and I should have been. But as circumstances would have it, I became more involved in church music. My granddad put me in charge of a youth music program to keep me encouraged. At times, my cousin Joann and I would stay at church after Sunday school to practice and to write songs. She played guitar and we prayed and sang until church in the evening.

Another cousin, Dale Puckett and I were very close as well. He and I wrote letters back and forth after his mother, Aunt Dorothy Jo and his dad divorced. He was living with his dad in South Carolina and had learned to play saxophone in the school band. Later, Dale moved to Washington, DC and along with his younger brother, Dwight, became members of my first country band. After my experience in Washington working for Earl Dixon, Dale, Dwight and my younger brother, Randy worked with me for a while in a country gospel group. I often joke about allowing Randy to learn to play bass at my expense. Once he got good enough he went on to work with Opry star, Jean Shepard and eventually in Dolly's short-lived family band. I never participated in the family act since I was already working on my own.

After the band with Dale, Dwight and Randy, I toured with the "Chaplain of Bourbon Street," evangelist, Bob

Harrington, working with tracks on a reel-to-reel tape recorder. I also toured with Dottie and the Singing Rambo's as a single act. Deciding I needed to put together a group like everyone else in gospel music I put together a folk gospel group with my sister, Cassie, Bobby Cox on piano and Clayton Head on bass and me on autoharp and percussion. We did four-part harmonies. We worked churches and almost starved. During this time, I worked as a hostess at the Red Lobster and worked churches on the weekends. Occasionally I performed on Jimmy Snow's Grand Ole Gospel show after the Opry went off the air on Friday nights. Also, Little Roy Wiggins' Saturday radio show aired live from his music store and the Ernest Tubb Midnite Jamboree on Saturday nights after the Opry. These shows gave me enough exposure to continue finding roadwork. At these appearances, I met lots of Opry stars and even the Pointer Sisters worked ET's Midnite Jamboree one night. That was a highlight for me. I loved their sound, their look and their style. Seeing them reminded me once again of what I thought my sisters and I could have been doing.

During this phase, I recorded a gospel album called "Stella and the Gospel Carrolls." I used that name after the family summit "on the name thing." Uncle Louis took me to Sumar Talent, a gospel-booking agency owned by J.D. Sumner and John Matthews. I don't recall ever getting a job through their agency. They didn't know what to do with me. Needless to say, neither of us benefited from the relationship. But Uncle Louis tried hard to make up for helping mess up my situation in Washington.

Uncle Louis even asked Carlton Haney to release a single from my album on his label, Music City Records, to give me product to sell on the road. Carlton Haney promoted Merle Haggard's tour and arranged for me to open for him. I also recorded a song with Johnny Bush called

"Toy Telephone." Johnny was with RCA, and Frank Dycus, a songwriter at Dolly and Porter's publishing company, suggested they use me on the record. I was thrilled. The song charted and eventually was covered by Tammy Wynette and George Jones with their daughter, Georgette, doing the little girl voice that I performed on Johnny's recording.

By this time, Uncle Louis owned his own record label, Royal American. He released another single for me from the same album, providing another 45 to sell at my shows. Not long after, Uncle Louis introduced me to Pete Drake. He agreed to produce two songs on me from Dolly's catalog – "Stranger" and "Old Black Kettle." Tommy Hill agreed to release these recordings. We arranged to sign a contract, and I was excited, hoping to secure record company support for my music. However, Pete told me backstage at the Opry on the Saturday night before I was to sign that I would need to do him a "personal favor" before he would release my project. I told him to "stick it where the sun don't shine." It would be another two years before another recording opportunity came along. I never told Uncle Louis about Pete's stipulations because I didn't want to cause trouble. I suppose Uncle Louis assumed my commitment to singing was not that strong, probably thinking I would give up and go to work in the beauty shop where he thought I belonged.

At one point, Dolly developed throat problems and was placed on complete vocal rest. She was ordered to write everything down to communicate; therefore, she was unable to sing on the Porter Wagoner show. In desperation, having no viable replacement, they called me. I filled in for her on a weekend trip to Ohio and Wheeling, West Virginia. On the way back home, Porter told me that he wanted to take me in the studio and produce a session on me. He thought I was talented and had a unique style. Needless to say, I was overjoyed.

Porter produced the session with the two songs he had chosen and secured permission to release it on RCA with the understanding that I would use the name "Stella." I agreed in the hallway of the RCA studios. After he played the session for Dolly, he asked me to come by his office on Monday morning and sign the contract. I called to nail down the time and was told Porter would call back. I am still waiting for a call back.

No one ever called or explained to me why Porter and RCA had changed their minds. I was crushed. I wondered if he had gone through that entire charade and expense to hurt Dolly. Regardless, I felt that I had been a pawn in his little power game with her. To add insult to injury, several months later Uncle Bill played my session with his girlfriend Kay's voice recorded over my tracks. He and Porter had taken my voice from the tracks and replaced it with hers. I began to withdraw from all of them. As Dr. Phil would say, some thirty or so years later, "What were they thinking?" Someone with less determination might have given up at this point, but not me.

After some time had passed, Uncle Louis called and offered me a job. When I wasn't working as a hostess at the Red Lobster, booking my group and singing in churches on the weekends, I worked part-time at Dolly and Porter's recording studio and publishing company as a reception-ist, filing and archiving press into scrapbooks. Uncle Louis ran the company and offered me the part-time job so that I could work out some time in the studio. He did this in lieu of paying me a salary.

However, I still had three mouths to feed, so I sold cars through the classifieds. My former manager, Earl Dixon, offered me a deal I couldn't refuse. It provided me a vehicle to drive, plus he allowed me to add to his set price so that I could make a little extra income. Once it sold, he would send another car and this kept me going one entire winter. One time, he sent a car that filled up with water when it rained. One night the floorboard turned into a huge block of ice when the temperature dropped. Darlene, my babysitter, and I frantically removed the ice before the buyer came to pick up his new wheels.

Whew! The joys of single motherhood and good ol' "love offerings" from friends and strangers. Darlene and I still laugh about rolling that big block of ice down the driveway before the buyer showed up. Lord, forgive us!

There were times I only had enough money from the "love offering" to pay the band and buy gas for the station wagon. Fortunately, I was blessed with a son who loved peanut butter and jelly, because he ate lots of it then. Macaroni and cheese became a specialty and still happens to be Tim's favorite "Mom" recipe.

After a couple of years of trying to integrate into Southern Gospel music, singing what now is called Christian Country, I felt I didn't belong there either. The churches I sang in were all kind to us, but didn't know what to make of my little group and me. Most of the Southern Gospel folks saw me as something else altogether. One night at a show, one well-known individual came right out and told me that I wasn't "one of them." I still don't understand that considering we are all God's children and I was only doing my part to praise the Lord. I was told, I was in the secular world and shouldn't be singing in churches. I still wonder who made them God. I suppose they were referring to the fact that I had been singing country music for a time.

Numerous people would say to me, "I bet your sister, Dolly, really supports your ministry." Based on this faulty assumption, they were extremely tight with "love offerings." But my bills came due every month just like everyone else's. Bob Harrington's Crusade took up offerings in two-gallon water buckets and I was being paid $150 out of which I paid 10% to my manager and covered expenses. I really would have been happy with just one bucket full, Bob! Bob was a popular evangelist at that time in the southeast.

As one of my many jobs, I sold Avon and cleaned Dolly's house. Because she was either on the road, in the studio, or at the publishing company when she was in town, she needed the help and I needed the money. Tim was two at the time and $45 a week was a blessing. I raked in the dough with my $45 from hostessing at the Red Lobster. A ninety-buck week with a nice ice-making car made life great. Topping it off with an occasional Shoney's hot fudge treat split three ways, and skin that was oh so soft from the Avon samples. But, oh, how I loved show business.

I once wrote a song about one of those cars. I called it, "Don't Get Too Close You'll Hurt Yourself." The idea came from the rust bucket I drove at the time. Mama gave me her little white station wagon to use on the road. This thing was also a rust bucket and the inside was worse. We spray-painted the floor in the back Swimming Pool Blue and tossed in a foam mattress to sleep on during long trips to and from those weekend shows.

Somebody told me I was paying dues, but it felt more like I was paying penitence for someone else's sin. The tougher things became the more determined I got. During this phase, Tim's dad and I finally divorced after a long separation. Hopelessness and despair became a frequent companion. But Tim was the brightest light in this dark time. His sparkling blue eyes and shining blonde hair colored my world oh so bright.

Around this time, I met a young guy from Missouri, Ron Woolman, who wanted to start booking me in clubs. Needing desperately to make more money, I decided to give country music another shot. Ron and I worked together only for a few months; however I was back working in clubs with house bands and doing a little better financially. Shortly thereafter, Shorty Lavender and Dick Blake, who owned their own booking agencies, booked my shows for a while. Then I signed with Joe Taylor's agency. Joe continued to book most of my shows throughout the coming years.

During the early seventies, I started writing truck-driving songs, since that was the preferred country music flavor at that time. Out of this songwriting phase I co-wrote with a musician and songwriting friend, Bob Dean, a song called, "Ode To Olivia" in response to everyone in country music being so upset because Olivia Newton-John won the Female Vocalist award at the CMA's that year. I loved her music and thought they were all overreacting. Dolly heard the song and asked me very sincerely to make sure Porter didn't hear it. That was the first time I realized she had to watch her step around him. But in protest, I told her to tell him to "piss off." "Ode To Olivia" got everyone's dander up for a while and I got a lot of coverage over it in country music publications and it even made the charts in Cash Box and Record World. Olivia's management called and said she wanted a dozen copies to send to her family in Australia. I was thrilled and eventually she and I met that same year at a function and she thanked me personally for being on her side. She was as nice as I had hoped she would be. Needless to say, I was known as a maverick of sorts during this period in my life. We also wrote a beautiful ballad, "I Want To Hold You In My Dreams Tonight," and in 1975, it became my first country hit. Although, I helped start the Soul, Country and Blues label these two songs were released on, financed the recording session, named the publishing company that published them, borrowed the money to finance the distribution, and hired the promotion guy, I never received one dime from its success. However, it gave me enough momentum to push me to the next level. Twenty years later, I bought back the publishing rights to the song.

After the chart success of the "I Want To Hold You In My Dreams Tonight" single, I went into the studio and worked on another album project. It was never officially released but was later sold to a small record company in Australia. I never finished my vocals, as we were still writing and changing the songs. Anyway, I don't know its eventual title, but two of the singles from it charted: "You've Crossed My Mind" and "The Mood I'm In." During this time, my agent, Joe Taylor, took me to Elektra Records. There I met Jim Malloy who was in charge of A&R (artist and repertoire) and he had produced artists like Sammi Smith, including her megahit, "Help Me Make It Through The Night."

Jim signed me to the label in 1976 and produced the three most successful albums of my recording career: "Country Sweet," "Love Ya," "Stella Parton," and the compilation, "The Best Of Stella Parton." Each song released from these albums became Billboard Chart Records, some making it to the Top 20 and Top 10: "I Want To Hold You In My Dreams Tonight," "Steady As The Rain," "I'm Not That Good At Goodbye," "Standard Lie Number One," "The Danger Of A Stranger," "The Room At The Top Of The Stairs," "Stormy Weather," "It's Not Funny Anymore," "You've Crossed My Mind," "Undercover Lovers," "Four Little Letters," "Young Love," "Cross My Heart," and "I Don't Miss You Like I Used To." "Danger Of A Stranger" was a hit in Great Britain and in 1978; I won Most Promising International Act at the Great Britain Country Music Award show in London.

When I signed with Elektra Records in 1976, I also hired a wonderful manager in Los Angeles, California. Norty Styne had grown up in the music industry as the son of Jules Styne, the songwriter whose hits included such classics as "Three Coins In A Fountain" and numerous others. Norty taught me a couple of valuable lessons including how to "work a talk show" and how to "speak to the press." Norty was a good person and I liked him. John McMeen booked my shows during this time and would continue to do so for a few more years, even acting as road manager whenever I needed him.

During my three-year tenure with the label, Jim Malloy and I married for a time. I learned some of the most valuable yet painful lessons from him both professionally and personally. No one should ever have to give up so much control over his or her own life. I may have walked into the Elektra office, but after three eventful years, I limped out or should I say, crawled out. That's all I want to say on the subject because it is still too painful.

After Elektra, I recorded a road album with four jazz musicians and they became my touring band. This album contained all original material, including songs I co-wrote with Paul Overstreet and Bob Teague. I still think of it as one of my truest pieces of work although it was never released commercially to radio. The album was appropriately called, "True To Me." People would come up after shows at this time during autograph sessions and say, "Stella, we don't know what kind of country music you're playing but we sure like it." The band was putting in all these jazz chords and I was learning how to improvise on the melodies. This kept the music fresh and exciting. We released "Legs," a novelty song, on an independent label called Wedge Records that got some airplay, but no Billboard chart action. No one in Nashville wanted to give me a second shot on a major label after the Elektra deal was finished. Music Row is still a small, close-knit group of "good ole boys." I had stood up for myself and "they would show me a thing or two," I was told by one disgruntled record executive.

Financially struggling again and no new recording contract on the horizon, I was offered an opportunity to play the lead in a musical, "Seven Brides For Seven Brothers" on the west coast. Wanting a chance to broaden my horizons, I took it. I had no idea what I was getting into. In rehearsal, I felt like I had gone from the frying pan into the fire, but with only nine days of rehearsal and no previous acting or dancing experience. Except for an episode of "The Dukes of Hazzard," my acting experience consisted of selling cars through the classifieds. I learned all the dance steps after being stepped on by my leading man in rehearsal and breaking a bone in my foot, all the music with a thirty-six-piece orchestra and all the dialogue. Luckily, I pulled it off with great reviews. I also learned how to sing "show tunes" instead of interpreting attitude songs. My confidence soared for the first time in a long while. Still, being very underweight, overworked and underpaid, I needed this validation to keep me going because I kept thinking maybe someone would see my musical potential and give me another shot with a recording contract.

Still touring with my band from the record success of the Elektra years, I received an offer to sign with New York label, Accord/Townhouse. My managers at the time jumped on the offer. Paired with Milan Williams, a member of the Motown group, the Commodores, we worked at the Hitsville/Motown Studios in Los Angeles. I learned so much musically from the experience. I began training my ear in the studio and felt I improved on my pitch and delivery. As I listen to this album today, I can hear a difference in my technique. I was grateful to have all the time I needed to get the performance as good as possible. Milan produced a very good album for me. He and I even co-wrote a few of the songs. This album was called "So Far So Good." Working with a Motown producer brought back my teenage love for the Detroit sound and I was so proud of the album.

I was out on tour promoting the album when I called the company's main office to see where my single had charted that week. I was informed that the record, "Young Love," had gone to #20 on the Billboard charts, but that I was no longer effectively on the label since it had "become insolvent." I guess they meant bankrupt! It was so difficult to get back on the bus and keep the bad news from the band. Keeping up morale of a show is one of the many jobs of an artist.

In June, I accepted a role in another musical - the part of "Miss Mona" in a bus/truck tour of "The Best Little Whorehouse In Texas." That deal turned bad when the producer defaulted on the contract. I ended up in arbitration in New York. The money owed me on the contract has yet to materialize, but the producer bought a farm with the money he made from the tour.

The next spring I hit the road again with a band to recoup some of the losses I had incurred. Due to the string of bad luck, I had to sell my house. Tim and I moved into a two-bedroom apartment.

By summer of that year, I had a physical breakdown and my face became paralyzed from Bell's Palsy on the right side for about three months. Finally, I came around after taking steroid shots, but I didn't perform for almost a year due to anxiety.

My brother, Randy, finally talked me into going back into the studio and he produced three beautiful songs on me. I released one – a wonderful song called "Cross My Heart," written by Randy, my sister Rachel and Frank Dycus - as a single and produced a video. Both the video and single charted, even though I had very little money to promote them.

Then in the spring of 1986, another theatrical production crossed my path: a production of "Pump Boys &
Dinettes" in Calgary, Canada. Spending the summer in
Canada and having seen the original production on Broadway, I was honored to have the chance to play "Rhetta" in
the show. After the production ended in Calgary, I came
back to Nashville a bit better off financially, so I decided to
go back in the studio.

It was about this time Dolly called and asked me to produce a couple of stage shows for Dollywood's first season.
Dollywood is a theme park in my hometown. The park is an
Appalachian version of Disneyland. Dolly is the spokesperson and the creative force. I hired a choreographer from
New York and a musical director and put together a couple shows for some of our family members. Also serving
as music consultant for the park, I got a good taste of the
corporate attitude of theme park life by attending meetings over the next two years and offering numerous sug-
gestions, many of which were implemented over the years.
This was rewarding, and I felt I had been able to contribute
to what Dolly was doing in a positive way. However, I was
grateful not to have to work in the park, with all the jeal-
ousy and resentment projected toward our relatives who
were singing there.

Steve Messer and I started writing together around
1987. Steve was a great sound engineer who had worked
on some demos I had done over the years. He and I started
work on another album project to shop around to the
labels in Nashville.

Frank Jones, who worked for Mercury Records, was now
with a new independent label, Airborne Records, and he
signed our project. Although we had a great piece of work,
they used all the investment money to sign and record a
number of other artists. Airborne never released the album

even though I was used to sell stock in the company; some-time later, I was told this by someone at the label. I had invited Dolly to sing a duet with me on a song from *Pump Boys and Dinettes* called, "Sisters." That was the only song they wanted to release. So much for the last name angle. It was working for everybody but me. Needless to say, the hurt and disappointment were severe. I thought, how dare they want to exploit my sister in order to promote the label not me as an artist. Eventually, I secured the masters from another company in Ireland that had bought the album from Airborne in the foreign markets. The album was called "Always Tomorrow." Steve and I did two more album projects, leasing them to labels in Switzerland and Scandinavia, but I didn't try to get them to radio in America knowing it would be a waste of time and money. The albums were "Picture In A Frame" and "Favorites, Vol. 1." There was no way I could compete with the major labels.

Again, Dolly called and asked me to serve as an Associate Producer on her network television show. She and I were happy to be working in tandem on another project and I was proud that the two I worked on were the highest rated of that season. She decided it would be a good idea to bring her publishing company back to Nashville from Los Angeles, if I would administer it for her. It took three years to pull the company back up to current standards due to the enormous body of work she has composed over the years. Fortunately, I had some very capable help and was pleased to again contribute to what I think is her most valuable artistic output. To me, Dolly is the greatest female writer of our time. I believe her songwriting is what people will most remember. It meant so much to me that she trusted me above everyone else with this important task.

Another musical came along, this time, an international tour of "Gentlemen Prefer Blondes." Enjoying this production more than any I had done so far, I felt like I created a completely new approach to the character, "Lorelei Lee." Also being flattered to play the role Marilyn Monroe had created in the film, I was grateful to get mostly good reviews.

In the early nineties, totally soured on the record business and most of the people in it, I decided to do my music my way and to market it to the people who had always bought it over the years. The internet was a wonderful "window of opportunity" for me.

Being inspired and snowed in for a few weeks alone in the mountains during the winter of 1994, I wrote another batch of songs. Over the next couple of years, I self-produced them as part of an album called "A Woman's Touch." This was the first time I recorded an album entirely of my own songs.

Over these last few years, I have appeared in a CBS Movie of the Week, "The Color Of Love," with Lou Gossett, Jr. and Gena Rowlands and have done some television commercials.

Along the way, I have written three cookbooks, and, due to their success, I appeared on the Home Shopping Network with my own natural food product line for a year. Lately I've received a number of awards within the independent music market. Meanwhile, I owned and operated a coffeehouse in 1994-1995 in my hometown of Sevierville, Tennessee. I produced and released another four albums through my production company, Attic Entertainment / Raptor Records. I served as National Spokesperson for the Christian Appalachian Project and currently conduct workshops for women who have been through domestic violence situations. I feel I am using all my life experiences in a positive way. Life is very good and I feel better about my career and myself than ever before. Just last year, I was conferred a Doctorate of Sacred Music from Emmanuel University and most recently a Doctorate of Humanities, presented at the Pentagon at the First Annual Gospel Music Jubilee.

I am still traveling with an all-girl band and doing concerts. After having toured with all male musicians for so many years, I thought it might be fun to have an all female show. I have met so many talented women in Nashville. Working with women musicians has turned out to be a very rewarding and nurturing experience. We talk about our kids, husbands, boyfriends and menopause and we pray together and emotionally support one another. I have so much for which to be thankful. I can truly say I am most at home when I'm "singin' for my supper." I believe that is what I was born to do.

As I've grown through life, I've had many people be jealous and mean to me because they think I have had a very cushy life. The truth is: I'm always working. It's important for me to be about my Father's business. It's like when they said to Jesus, "Where have you been?" And he said, "Well, I have been about my father's business." Yet some people have been envious and cruel to me even though I have never stopped working for a day. I've noticed that people who work the least seem to be the most miserable. I have also learned to try to avoid those folks. Well, God has blessed me, but he has blessed me mostly with courage, a fearless nature and determination. I'm probably as determined as anyone could ever be. I have never been that well off financially, but I have been so blessed with the ability to make a lot out of a little. My dad was the same way. He could stretch a nickel as far as most people can stretch a dollar.

I don't know how many days I have here. Every day I waste is a day I won't get back. That goes for wasting time on relationships with those who can be mean and cruel.

A few years ago, I was having dinner with a promoter who has promoted country music for as long as I've been in the business. He is in a position to help people if he so chooses. I had been doing some shows for him, so he invited me to dine with him one evening at one of the big, fine restaurants in Nashville. This man wore a toupee, lots of gold jewelry, and those big Elvis glasses from the early 70s. He looked like Howard Cosell dressed up like Elvis.

All through dinner, he belittled me by telling me I needed to get my breasts enlarged and so forth. I just listened and tried to make light of it as much as possible. I've gotten used to this type of attitude over the years. I just try to consider the source.

He continued to tell me that my sister, Dolly, was the sexiest, most intelligent woman in the business and I would never be able to compare with her because I was too conservative. He thought I was over the hill anyway and had wasted most of my time when I should have dressed in skimpy outfits and been more outrageous when I was younger. He thought I should have been more of an attention-getter.

All the while, I was thinking, "What does that have to do with my singing?" He really was feeling good about himself while verbally berating me. But then, as I looked up from my plate of spaghetti, he bit down on a fork full of steak and one of the front teeth in his new shiny white dentures fell out. I was really proud of myself for not laughing. It was a true miracle that I was able to hold myself together. I've thought about that often when people are rude and nasty to me. Actually, I then began to feel sorry for him, so I played it down by telling him you could hardly see it in that darkened restaurant.

Every day we allow someone else to waste is a day we allow to be stolen from us. And that day will never be restored. Yet, we can't hold grudges. I just try to keep a sense of humor about it all.

I guess people do the best they can with what they have to work with. If you don't believe it, look at me. I try to start my day out with a prayer and to be thankful. Then I try to forgive everyone I need to, and I even thank God for the mean people. If things were great all the time, we wouldn't have the opportunity to learn much about ourselves or about life, now would we?

I've learned in the last few years that if I'm going to be miserable in a situation, I need to take a good honest look at myself, my actions, thoughts and attitudes. First, I start to work on my attitude and adjust that. Then my thoughts just follow my attitude, and before I know it, my actions begin to fall in line. It's as if I've suddenly had an Alka-Seltzer and a chiropractic adjustment all at once. I let my thoughts be praise, and even the worst day turns out okay.

Try it. You might like it. No, I'm *sure* you'll like it.

Listen, if the phoenix can recreate itself once from the ashes and if it has that much power, then why wouldn't it have the power to do it many, many times? As many times as necessary.

We experience rebirth often during our lifetime. And each time, hopefully, we become stronger and better able to balance ourselves. Life is never on the flat line until we die.

Between now and then, let's ride that line, even if it's like a roller coaster – dealing with the downs and savoring the ups. There's no way around it, so let's take the walk through the valleys on our way to reach the peaks.

All of us have a bit of the phoenix in us and we need to use it to our advantage as we improve and enjoy our lives. If we can't get over something or under it and there's no way to get through it, for goodness sake, just go around it. Besides, as Hunter S. Thompson would say – *"The music business is a cruel and shallow money trench, a long plastic hallway where thieves and pimps run free, and good men die like dogs. There's also a negative side."*

miracles

Me and my handsome son, Tim, all grown up.
(Photo by Rose Mason / Courtesy of the Attic Entertainment Archives)

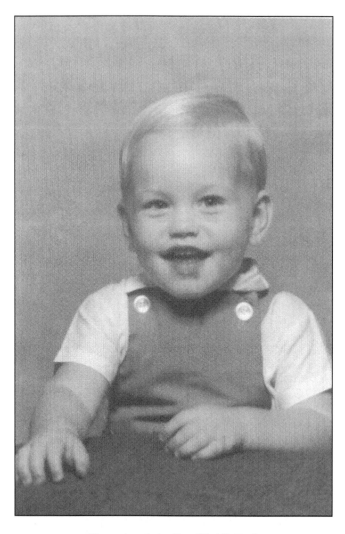

My precious baby, Tim. ("Toddle Tim")
(Courtesy of the Attic Entertainment Archives)

Me and Tim at his swearing in ceremony for the
Tennessee State Bar. Yeah, I'm a proud mom!
(Courtesy of the Attic Entertainment Archives)

Me and Tim at my AACC Graduation Ceremony at the Opryland Hotel.
(Courtesy of the Attic Entertainment Archives)

Me at my lowest weight. Those jeans were actually loose.
(Courtesy of the Attic Entertainment Archives)

On a fishing trip. Yes, I put my own worm on the hook.
(Courtesy of the Attic Entertainment Archives)

"The Parton Girls"(left to right): Freida, Dolly, Willadeene, Rachel, Me and Cassie.
(Courtesy of the Family Archives)

Performing at the Hat House Café Parlor Show.
(Courtesy of the Attic Entertainment Archives)

My favorite stage clothes.
(Courtesy of the Attic Entertainment Archives)

Every hillbilly woman needs to know how to drive a pick-up truck.
(Courtesy of the Attic Entertainment Archives)

Signing autographs at a show.
(Courtesy of the Attic Entertainment Archives)

My new hair-do.
(Courtesy of the Attic Entertainment Archives)

Showing nerves right before going on stage.
(Courtesy of the Attic Entertainment Archives)

A couple of my character looks for acting jobs.
(Courtesy of the Attic Entertainment Archives)

Me and my trusty left-handed Martin.
(Photo by Brenda Madden / Courtesy of the Attic Entertainment Archives)

*A few of the most important people who
have been invaluable throughout my career.*

Darlene Williams Tatum getting Tim ready for a show.
(Courtesy of the Attic Entertainment Archives)

Brenda Madden and Me attending a celebration for a friend.
(Courtesy of the Attic Entertainment) Archives)

*Me and Johnny Cochran, who has always been one of
my most supportive fans as well as a dear friend.*
(Courtesy of the Attic Entertainment Archives)

Me and John Elbirn at one of our many Fan Fair functions.
(Courtesy of the Attic Entertainment Archives)

Joe Taylor and Me. I'm presenting Joe with a
"Top Hat" Award of Appreciation.
(Courtesy of the Attic Entertainment Archives)

Brant Moll, Me and Bill Reid attending the
Ralph Stanley birthday celebration.
(Courtesy of Coal News Newspaper)

Me in one of my more serious moods.
(Photo by Sean Woodbury / Courtesy of the Attic Entertainment Archives)

Yes, it's true, I can be a "Southern Belle."
(Photo by Brenda Madden / Courtesy of the Attic Entertainment Archives)

Autographing after a show.
(Courtesy of the Attic Entertainment Archives)

"Learn to get in touch with the silence within yourself. There's no need to go to India or somewhere else to find peace. You will find it in your room, your garden or even your bathtub."
– Elisabeth Kühler-Ross

The Good Book And Other Good Books

I've always loved the way a book *feels*, the way a book *smells*, and just to *see* bookshelves, and libraries. It's like that line in a John Denver song, *"You fill up my senses."* Oh, just give me a book. Books are so magical.

The first book I read that made an impression on me was <u>Ben Hur</u>. My Aunt Estelle gave it to me as a Christmas gift. She bought us a lot of books, as we all loved to read.

<u>Ben Hur</u> was the coolest story for a ten-year old child to read. It came alive in my mind. In school you're studying and being taught from the teacher's point of view and doing your lessons. This, however, provided a refreshing escape from all that. No teacher assigned this; I chose this adventure into a world I knew nothing about. What a miraculous discovery! I read the entire book over the

Christmas holidays, and from then on, I am always reading at least two or more books at a time.

Even now, as I get up in the morning, I make my coffee and read from a devotional book. Since I became old enough to wear reading glasses, the first things I do is brew my coffee and then look for reading glasses so I can start reading. When I'm not working, I read ninety percent of my down time. When you think about it, that makes my *down* time my *up* time. All these years, I read textbooks to educate myself. While the band on the bus was playing cards or watching videos, I read in the back. Oprah's book club doesn't have a thing on me. I've read Hemingway, Fitzgerald, Faulkner, Grisham, Conroy, Morrison and Angelou. Oh, did I mention Lorian Hemingway; the list is too long to mention them all. I'll never live long enough nor read fast enough to read everything I have on my own shelves.

I'm reading books on marketing now, such as *Words That Sell* by Richard Bayan. I'm not sure about other languages, but English has a lot of catch phrases and trendy words that are constantly overused. As a child, words such as "far out" and "cool" were common. Now "awesome" is the big deal and "whatever" has taken the stage. Anyway, I recommend this fabulous book.

After reading about every self-help book out there, I can safely say that one of my favorites remains *The Power Of Positive Thinking* by Norman Vincent Peale. I'm reading it again. A second reading often opens new avenues and I encourage second and even third reads on important works.

Some of the more recent titles I've read: *The Incomplete Education* by Judy Jones and William Wilson, a huge volume covering everything from philosophy to religion, history, literature and psychology. It's just a short synopsis on these subjects but it's fun to discover a new point of view. I think it was given to me as a joke because of my inferiority complex about my education. I'm reading a book on the aging process at the moment and learning how to enjoy the benefits of aging instead of dwelling on the down side of growing old. Who are they trying to kid? *Growing Younger* by Bridget Doherty and Julia Van Tine advises how to adjust to the aging process in a positive way. Meanwhile, I'm reading a book on cures found in nature – Michael Castleman's *Nature's Cures*. Lord, I hope they have some definitive answers. I'm going down hill fast. Here is the bottom line: We're gonna live 'til we die. So don't sweat it.

Nevertheless, you know, I can't read novel after novel, although I read lots of them. I must keep up with Oprah! I love autobiographies, not just because it's fluff reading, but because it's another way to examine how others became successful. What were the personality traits that propelled them to success? The extreme highs and extreme lows of these famous people who have made an impact on the world. Thomas Jefferson, Abraham Lincoln, Winston Churchill, Will Rogers, Jimmy Carter, Martin Luther King, Jr. …and the list goes on and on.

I read books that help me with whatever stage I'm going through. When I feel an urge to learn something new, I head for the bookstore or the library. I also love libraries. Books are the most incredible gifts we have in our society. We can go to the library, get on the computer and find anything we want – books, magazines, videos, even compact discs. There is absolutely no excuse for not finding information. There's no excuse for not using information.

Of course, the best book is the Good Book. I own many different Bibles and Bible reference books because one is not enough. I compare one to the other. I'm reading the Book of Esther from the *Living Bible,* which is kind of modern speech, then I go back and read the King James Version.

I read that book of the Bible three times in one week. Did you know there are only two books in the Bible that have women's names? Aside from Esther, the other is Ruth. I guess that's because women weren't allowed to learn to read and write. We're also supposed to be seen and not heard. "Whatever." Sure am glad to live in America.

Although miracles abound throughout the Bible, I am particularly fond of the Book of Esther. The greatest miracle I learned from the Book of Esther is how she began as an orphan, was adopted and then became Queen. To go from being an orphan, then being adopted and later becoming the queen and ultimately saving your people! That's quite a miracle. She never gave up, and neither should you. If you do then, you might miss being a queen, king or at the very least happy and fulfilled.

Read the Book of Corinthians or the Book of Proverbs, any time you need to get practical information on how to live your life and how to apply the wisdom to what's going on in your life from day to day. Both books provide timeless lessons for daily living not just for the ancients, but also for us today.

What this teaches is that human nature remains constant. No matter what's going on, we still react the same way to the same things as did people of old. We have telephones and cars, but emotionally we have not advanced.

God deals with our hearts and emotions. That is what the Holy Spirit is. We must deal with God on that same level – through our spirit. It's why He calls us His children and says we need to be like children in our hearts. That's what the Bible is trying to teach us. What a miracle! Very simple, yet with our ego, we try to complicate it by acting as if we have it all figured out.

"Masterpieces have a strange air of simplicity."
– *Virginia Woolf*

The Plan Of Salvation

A distant cousin and minister friend of mine, the Reverend James Parton, was blind for much of his life. He was the most devout Christian I ever knew. For some reason, he just chose to love me. As I was growing up, he would go preach at other churches. I'd go with him and be the singer, opening the service before his preaching.

He came to see me baptized at the age of fifty in the Little Pigeon River. He couldn't see with his eyes, but he just had to be there for the occasion. Family members brought him and stood with him outside the car. He was then quite elderly and frail. It meant so much to me to have him there. Although I had been baptized when I was a child, I wanted to be re-baptized for my own reasons as an adult because it was truly my decision and not someone elses.

James never owned a home or a car, and his wife Ila never had any children. I'll always remember how each time he met someone for the first time, he would ask, "Are you a Christian?" He was such a blessing to people in the church and the community because of his sweet and innocent personality.

There was always such love in his heart for everyone. He was not a scholar by any means, but he had a great capacity to love everyone. He had become a Christian while he was still a teenager in one of my Granddad's revival meetings, and felt the call to go into the ministry. Although he never pastored a church, he continued to preach throughout his life. He conducted funerals, weddings, revivals and home-coming services and he visited the sick. There was always someone to drive him wherever he felt the need to go.

The message of his ministry was the simple plan of sal-vation. "For God so loved the world that he gave his only begotten son that whosoever believeth on him should not perish but have everlasting life." He preached the third chapter of John his whole life and never missed a chance to ask strangers if they were Christian. James was so inno-cent he never noticed if they were shocked or offended by his asking. He witnessed the same message wherever he went – to doctors, nurses, the meter reader, the grocery store clerk – it didn't matter to James.

James' wife was his biggest supporter. Although she held a regular job cleaning rooms in Gatlinburg, she never missed a church service, prayer meeting or hospital visit. She was right beside him in every effort he made to preach and witness to the people of our community.

His great desire was to have me there when he died. I, too, wanted to be there. I knew he would be rejoicing the entire time. I didn't want to miss it. He and Ila had prayed I would be there when his time came. I had seen them not very long before he died and we had the most wonderful visit. Before I left, we all prayed together.

The night he died, I was out of town and could not be reached. For some reason his wife Ila just happened to walk out into the hall of the hospital and saw my sister Willadeene. My sister didn't know they had taken James to the hospital as she was there visiting someone else. Willadeene is one of those earth angels I keep mentioning. She walked into his room and touched him just as he called my name. Willadeene rang me later and told me how beautiful his passing had been. She went on to say the sweetest thing anyone has ever said to me: "Stella, I was honored to be there in your place."

I see this as a miracle for me, for James, Ila and my sister. Because of love, we were all spiritually connected in such a special moment in time. I know where you are, James. And I don't ask, "Are you a Christian?" I don't need to.

"A good feeling inside is worth more than a great beautician."

– Mother Teresa

All Dressed Up And Somewhere To Go

S top looking for Jesus to turn water into wine. Stop looking for the earth to stop spinning and the moon to turn to blood.

Look at the miracle of life and the love people give out like those firefighters, police officers and rescue workers at the Twin Towers on September 11, 2001. Like the priest who died while offering last rites to a victim of the terrorist attack on the World Trade Center. Is that not a miracle? What a way to go! The Reverend Mychal Judge, 68 years old, was a charismatic Franciscan Catholic priest, who loved, lived and died serving as the Chaplain of the New York Fire Department. While kneeling over, administering last rites to a dying firefighter, falling debris killed him. What a great miracle for him, one he so richly deserved – to meet our Lord in such a precious and heroic way at that very saintly moment.

It's like the miracle of my Aunt Estelle, one of the sweetest and most giving human beings I ever knew. She's the one I'm named for. She gave to all our family – not just my mom and dad, but my brothers and sisters as well. It was just her nature to be loving. She and her husband, Uncle Dot, were childless, but they helped rear everyone else's children. She took care of Grandma, Grandpa, and anyone else who needed it.

When Aunt Estelle died in her 70's, God let her have such a peaceful transition. She had had her hair and nails done that very day. When she got home, my uncle was in his recliner, and she lay down on the sofa as they watched the evening news together. She fell asleep. Later that night he went over to wake her up, and she was gone.

That's a miracle. God took her in her sleep. All dressed up and ready to go to a party, and what a party to which she was going! She couldn't have had it any better. She deserved to go peacefully. She never suffered and needed no one to care for her. She never wanted to be cared for. She was that kind of angel.

It's a miracle God let my Aunt Estelle meet him all dressed up and in peace. There was no struggle. God and my Uncle Dot were right there with her. She died exactly where she would have wanted to be – on her own sofa with my uncle right there beside her.

No one ever said a bad word about my Aunt Estelle. I did not attend the funeral. I stayed with my mom that day so everyone else could go. When my dad came home, I asked him how she looked. He said in his soft gentle voice with all the love and respect he always had for her, "She looked just like the angel she always was, not a bit different."

> *"Dying is the final stage of growth in life. The self, or spirit –
> or whatever you wish to label it – is eternal."*
>
> – *Mary Elisabeth Kübler-Ross*

Sometimes It's Hard To Say I Love You

I had a big fight once with a woman who later became my friend. Maggie was a much older lady who had lived a rowdy life, married a wealthy older man when she was in her forties, and had one child. Her husband died, but left her well off with a trust fund for her son, whom she raised alone. She ran through a lot of the money though, drinking much of it away. When her son was in high school, Maggie suffered a debilitating stroke and had to learn how to walk and talk again.

We met when I was living in an apartment complex that she managed. I was about 23, pretty feisty, and didn't know how to behave properly. (I still don't know how to behave – but I *really* didn't know how back then.) I discovered that when I was out of town working Maggie was showing my apartment to prospective tenants as a model.

I felt very violated when the maintenance man told me she was showing my place to total strangers without my consent. She should have used her own apartment, or somebody else's, as a model. Feeling very angry and violated, I marched over to her office in front of customers trying to rent apartments. I jumped all over her and let her have it. I lost it because I was very angry – it's a wonder she didn't throw me out after that scene in her office. Instead, she took a liking to me, for some reason. To my benefit, I think she admired my spunk. It was my lucky day. My temper has not usually served me well. I've learned when you give a piece of your mind to somebody; it's a piece you don't get back. Eventually, I realized I didn't have enough mind to give away.

Somehow, we became friends, and as the years went by, we remained very close. She was such a character. Although she no longer drank heavily, she smoked a lot. Nevertheless, she was my little buddy, I loved her, and she grew to love me even though she could never bring herself to say, "I love you." In an odd sort of way, she was like a mother figure to me, yet also a girlfriend. When we'd say goodbye after visiting each other, I would always hug her. She always kept her arms down by her sides and never hugged me back.

I would say, "Maggie, I love you." Yet, she couldn't say it back or even hug me in return. Over the years, gradually, she began to expect that hug. If I was busy or something, she would linger around until I finished whatever I was doing so that I could hug her. I thought she was doing this for me, so I would always hug her, saying, "Maggie, I love you. I'll talk to you later. Bye." She never could say those three words that mean so much and should be easy to say.

Years later, after she could no longer work from old age and illness, she moved into a retirement place. I'd visit her there and always hug her and say, "Maggie, I love you."

Even after we had been friends for so long, she just couldn't say it. Finally one day, she said, "Me, too." It sure felt good to hear her say that. Eventually, she started hugging me back. That was a big breakthrough, and I loved it.

As Maggie grew older, she moved to another state with her son, and ended up in a wheelchair as her health declined. Her son called me from the hospital the night she was dying. "Stella, Maggie wants to talk to you, and I knew you would want to speak to her - it's almost time," he said. "She wants to tell you goodbye."

On the other end of the phone, I could hear her in what they call in the mountains, "the death rattles." I thought, oh, it *is* time! It was very sad for me. Even though we had totally different personalities and completely different backgrounds, she was a very special friend to me. It had been my mission through all those years of friendship to get her to say, "I love you."

Her son put the phone to her ear, and I heard those chilling death rattles again. I said, "Oh, Maggie, wait until you get to Heaven, it's going to be so beautiful there and when I get there, make sure you have on that beautiful yellow dress I always love to see you wear. You always look like sunshine to me in that dress. I want to make sure we sit down and have a glass of your sweet iced tea by the pool." We always sat by the pool and drank ice tea. She loved open-toed high heels, so I added, "I'll make sure to wear my highest heels for you."

I was trying to be light, and at the same time, assuring her I would see her in Heaven. "Maggie, I sure hope you can hear me. I want you to know how much I love you."

And in her soft, weak voice, I heard her say, "Stella, I love you, too."

It had taken almost 20 years for her to say those words. Almost 20 years! It's hard to describe how those three

words coming from her made me feel. I believe I had a purpose in her life and finally she realized how important she
had been to me.

And those were the last words Maggie spoke.

"The hardest thing is learning some things about ourselves that we don't especially want to know."

– Ann Kaiser Stearns

Born Naked

I know a man who is basically a decent person but over the years somehow slipped into a negative mindset. He brags about his ability to impress people with his money and charm, and because of this, he claims he is able to get women or whatever he wants.

After my last discussion with him, I began to think about how some people believe that love is something you can buy or love is something you possess.

Love to me is none of these, because God is love. Real love is something you have to give away in order to keep. There's no bargain you can make with it and there are no deals. It's strange how some people get the idea that because they're born into wealth, privilege or beauty, they deserve better treatment than the rest of us. In fact, we're all the same when it comes down to being born. We all come into this world screaming and naked, and most of us go out of here gasping and usually naked except for a little gown opened down the back. Birth and death are the great equalizers.

> *The truth of the matter is, it's all a game*
> *Some liked the playing, some place the blame*
> *Some play by the rules, others played the fool*
> *The truth of the matter is, it's all a game.*

"The Truth of the Matter"
Written by: Stella Parton
©1995. My Mama's Music (BMI)

Throughout my life experiences, I've known many wealthy people. They all realize at the very end the most important thing, and it doesn't have anything at all to do with their money. I've known many poor people who have lived successful lives as human beings, realizing the real true meaning of life, knowing it was about being honest, about loving their family. These individuals knew about loyalty, being fearless, and having courage in the face of despair. They understood everything it took to make them extremely successful human beings.

It boils down to being quiet long enough to hear your own self. We should not get so much chaos going on. So much confusion in our life will keep us from getting in touch with who we really are. We create this distortion in our lives, like static on the radio, until we can't even discover who we are.

We all have clutter to deal with, but we need to surrender to love. Give up all the pretense and shallowness, and get down to *the truth of the matter*.

It saddened me when I left my last meeting with a prestigious, successful businessman.

I told him to his face. He started complaining about his daughter, telling me how she was wild and rebellious. He told me she had recently had a baby and he was not able to accept it. His reason was that he was embarrassed at the Country Club in front of his friends. He went on to tell me she had also had a number of abortions that she and her mother had kept from him. He made such statements while looking me straight in the face. I was stunned that he was so misguided at his age. He believed those statements and it saddened me even more.

Finally, I could take it no more and I spoke up and said, "Well, thank God your daughter finally came to her senses and has decided to live her own life regardless of what you think." My scolding shocked him. He called me a brassy broad. "Who do you think you are to be so brash?" he said.

Irritated, I shot back, "Who do you think you are to be so arrogant? I'm stunned at how you've allowed your ego to get in the way of your intellect. We're talking about the life of your grandchild, idiot."

But no one is a hopeless case. God has as much mercy on him as he does on anyone else because everyone is a child of God. It's like the story in the Bible about the prodigal son. God has compassion for us all because we are all his children. It's not for us to make that judgment. Thank goodness, that's the case, because I would have been in trouble. I would have smacked him over the head. However, it's not up to me; it's up to God to make that decision. There's no distinction, because God loves him just as I love my child. Who are we to say who is going to be saved and who are we to even dare to feel godly enough to make that distinction?

I've known people like him who have turned their lives around. Usually, it's something very devastating. I hope he realized what I was saying and that something sunk into his consciousness. I'm gonna pray about it for both of us.

One summer I was out on the road working fairs. We had done two shows and had just loaded up the bus. It was raining that night. There's nothing nastier than two shows at a fair on a muddy racetrack, everyone getting in and out of the bus. Tim was about 12 years old at this time and he was on the road with me. I was sitting up in the front of the bus and we were about to pull away when someone came to the door and said, "Is Stella on the bus?" The bus driver said, "Yes, but we're getting ready to leave."

Before the driver could say another word, this person bounded onto the bus so quickly we were all taken aback. When he got up the steps and into the lounge and onto a seat, he swiveled himself on a chair. We suddenly realized he had no legs and only one arm, but was able to maneuver himself so quickly. He was so agile for a man in this condition. He was young and nice looking. He said he wanted to meet me and to talk with me.

It turned out to be such an incredible visit as he told his story. He's an artist, painting with his one hand. He travels in a specially outfitted motor home that he drives himself. He told us he attempted suicide when he was a teenager because of a very abusive childhood. He threw himself in front of a speeding train, and that was how he lost three limbs. Somehow, he had survived and had rehabilitated himself.

God had a purpose for his life, and that was to witness to people like us. There we were, feeling miserable, overworked and underpaid. We were dirty, and it was muddy, yet who were we to complain? We had at least been out there on stage and people were applauding for us. Maybe we did have to drive another 500 miles on a moving vehicle and do another setup and another show the next day. And maybe we had done one the night before the same way. And maybe we were totally road-weary and exhausted. But who were we to complain? We could sit around and get the "poor-me's" about our situation. The first thing to do while we're feeling so sorry about ourselves is to get up off our butts and go down to a nursing home, a cancer ward, prison or even a leukemia ward at a hospital. Have you ever been to a burn unit in a hospital?

I never saw the man again and I do wonder what ever happened to him. I have never forgotten this experience. Maybe he was one of those earth angels who came by to say, "Here we are. We're all in this together."

Today when I was on a ten-mile hike, it came to me that I wanted to share this story. You don't have to look any farther than the end of your own arm to see someone worse off. You can touch somebody who may be in worse shape in one way or another.

Several years ago, I went to the women's prison in Nashville for a show. I was shocked to realize these women could be any of us. I remember one woman in particular. She was a grandmother in her seventies. After forty years of physical, mental and verbal abuse from her alcoholic husband, she snapped one night and killed him. She shot him and blew him all the way into the kitchen, the same kitchen where she had cooked his meals and fed his children since they were a young married couple. She could have been anyone's sweet little grandmother with white hair and a perm. I never forgot her. I sometimes wonder what happened. Did she die there? Life had been so horrible in her own home. How sad to end up this way. It could be anyone given similar circumstances.

"Until you've lost your reputation, you never realize what a burden it was or what freedom really is."

– *Margret Mitchell*

Close Encounters Of The Worst Kind

By the time I was 23 years old, I found myself divorced with a small baby to care for and was at the same time helping to raise my five younger siblings. I had a gospel group and was trying diligently to make my living as a gospel singer.

Daily, I found myself bombarded with the hypocrisy of so many people. One night I was so down and out about it I literally sat in my living room, feeling like a total failure. The way I was brought up, divorce was one of the ultimate sins. My thoughts and my opinion of myself turned very dark. I'm totally ruined. I'm ruined for life. I just might as well go ahead and kill myself because nobody is ever going to respect or love me again. I had been brought up to think, "Am I good enough yet, God? Am I good enough yet, God? I'm a good girl and I try to do right."

We're never going to be good enough for God to love us. God loves us just because he loves all his children.

That night I sat there in total despair thinking about my three-year-old baby, I wondered what would happen to him if I killed myself. I realized that other people would have to raise him and I would never know how he would grow up.

Suddenly it came to me that God gave Tim to me not because I was perfect, but as a mother, in most ways I think Tim is perfect and I can't help but love him. So if I love Tim that much, then how much more does God love us all? I guess that's what unconditional love is all about.

It makes no difference what other people think of me. It only matters what God thinks of me, and what I think of me.

The suicide thoughts ran very deep that night. I was devastated because I felt like such a failure – when, in fact, it wasn't my failure at all. It was one of my life lessons. Understanding the lesson also allowed me the opportunity to be a much better parent. I was charged at that point with the responsibility of being a stronger and better mother. In many ways, I became not only a mother but also a father to my son.

I have always gone through every phase of emotion trying to work out those choices I made. Although I never considered suicide again, I have certainly been heartsick each time and felt betrayed. You may judge me and ask why I failed so many times. I guess you could say I'm too trusting or just gullible. The truth is, I didn't know any better. I hope I've finally learned to set some boundaries. I have to take full responsibility for my choices. I have learned some hard lessons. I believe it's true that a divorce is as painful as a death. I think in some ways it's worse. If I ever attempt marriage again, I will certainly go to counseling and take my time in making such a decision. I have pantyhose that have lasted longer than my marriages. I assure you I am not making light of this situation, but that is funny. It's better to laugh than to cry about it. I hope I've learned something from it all. The more I think about it the more I think maybe I should have been a nun after all. Just kidding.

At one point in my life, I found myself involved in an abusive relationship with a man from a foreign country. I wasn't quite sure how to get out of it because he had me so terrorized I was afraid he would hurt Tim or Dolly because of our family being well known. I didn't think he would hurt me other than what he was already doing to abuse me. I was mainly worried he would have Tim or Dolly kidnapped. I was afraid to tell anyone about what was going on during this time. Therefore, I just kept going along with the relationship.

At one point, he had driven me out on tour while the band was traveling in another vehicle. He kept me in the car. I would do the show then get back into the car with him, and we would go to the next town. The main reason he was doing this was because I was trying to leave him. He wasn't going to allow this to happen because he had decided I was going home with him to visit his relatives through the holidays. I had been trying to break up with him for several months and could not figure out a way to get away from him.

This is another reason I understand how abusive situations can happen to women. And how you try to protect other people who might get hurt. Tim didn't know any of this was going on because he was at the military school, which was only 20 or 30 minutes from our house on the lake. But here was this man holding me hostage in my own home and traveling with me on the road. I couldn't get away from him and didn't know how to get the police to help me. This went on for several months.

The afternoon before we left, he accused me of trying to call someone to help me. He became so enraged he pulled the phone out of the wall, wrapped the cord around my neck and threatened to kill me if I ever left him. He was convinced that I was supposed to marry him.

We got to the airport in Nashville and I tried to get away from him but I was afraid I would embarrass my family. I didn't want to have him arrested in Nashville because it would be on the local news if I caused a scene at the airport. I decided I'd try to escape from him in the next big city, but I couldn't escape from him there either.

The next stop was out of the country, so I thought I'd get away from him there. At the hotel, he went to take care of some business, thinking I was far enough away from home that it would be safe to leave me alone. While he was gone, I caught a cab and rushed back to the airport. Just as I was getting in line to board the plane, he and one of his cronies came and pulled me out of the line.

I made a scene, but no one in the airport came to my assistance. No one. They just assumed it was a domestic issue and didn't want to get involved.

I found myself taken out of the country against my will. For ten days, I was with his family who did not speak a word of English. I kept praying and felt sure God would help me somehow. When he was out of the house one day, I thought that was my chance to escape, that someone had to help me. I started speaking to his mother through eye contact because neither of us understood a word of the other's language. We all talk so much we don't realize we have all these other ways of communicating. My eyes were all I had to speak with but I had to get my feelings across. I looked into her face and talked silently, communicating through eye-to-eye contact. I figured she was a mother and would understand my situation. Intuitively, she knew there was something wrong and I was not supposed to be there.

I begged her through my eyes, "Please, help me. You have to help me!" She saw that I was terrorized and, knowing I was from a well-known family in America, she suddenly became frightened her son was getting himself into a lot of trouble, as well as their entire family. So she did the mom thing. She took over.

That night when my kidnapper came home, they had a big fight. They had the loudest mouth-calling battle, but I didn't understand a single word they were shouting at each other. I can only guess what she was saying to her son.

The next morning, he took me to the airport and put me on a plane. That was the last time I saw him. Again, I was saved from a horrible situation. And that's another reason why I say God always sent an angel. His own mother became an angel for me at a critical point in time. And God gave me another miracle in being able to express myself perfectly without a single word.

Once a few years ago, I was waiting for a flight home at Heathrow Airport in London. A Middle Eastern man walked in with his family. There were several children of varying ages and at least five wives who also ranged in age. I was stunned when I noticed what looked like the youngest of the wives, carrying a small baby. This young woman was wearing a muzzle over her face. It was made of leather strips. I could not believe this type of abuse was going on in public view. Everyone in this family was acting as if it was normal except for her. She looked like a trapped animal. I so wanted to help her, but all I could do was pray. I will never be able to get this out of my mind. I pray for the women and children of this world every day. God have mercy on us. Seeing this reminded me of the horrible experience I had had years earlier.

People think angels are celestial beings with haloes hovering over their heads and wings poking out of their backs. In fact, there's a band of angels walking around, maybe with dirty faces and ragged clothes, right in your own neighborhood.

Sometimes you can see the angels and other times you can just feel them. A good loyal, loving friend you can depend on is an angel. It might be a brother or a sister - or a teacher or just a friend. I've had many teachers who have done angelic things for me. We've all had angelic things happen to us.

We have the opportunity at any given moment to become angels or perform angelic acts ourselves. I do my best to try to be an angel from time to time when I see a need. My intentions are to try to be what I call an earth angel as much as I know how to be. And what better way to feel like a day has not been a waste! If I can't be productive in one way, I'll try another way. Either I'll be creative, or maybe, instead, I can just be a blessing. Being a blessing in someone else's life is to make an angelic effort.

At the same time, I can turn right around and get into a major altercation at the drop of a hat. We do, after all, live on this planet in this realm, so we can't expect to live in the spirit all the time. There's no way we can because we live in a human form. In one sense, this form is the imperfection of life since our bodies are imperfect and only serve as vehicles to carry our souls around. We're spiritual beings – we just have human form.

I have a real problem with folks being so egotistical, claiming their religion is the only religion, and all others happen to be wrong. *"Beware of the teachers of the law. They like to walk around in flowing robes and love to be greeted in the marketplaces and have the most important seats in the synagogues and the places of honor at banquets. They devour widows' houses and for a show make lengthy prayers. Such men will be punished most severely." (Luke 20:46-47)* All of the religions I have read about are looking for the same thing. And that is love. They all are looking for God. It's all about trying to do good and be good. After all, the Bible says God is love. God is good. So let's be good.

I don't care what another person believes as long as he or she is trying to be a good person. Who can tell me they have met anyone who has made a roundtrip to Heaven, spent a few weeks there on vacation and then come back to tell us all about it? I'll just leave it up to God. We have to take it all on faith anyway. Men wrote the Bible and every other religion. But miracles are evidence of God's power.

Our children can be some of our best teachers. One time when Tim was small, I was really bummed out and having a bad day. Remember when we used to see those yellow and black happy face signs all the time, and "Have A Nice Day?" I saw the happy face sign as Tim and I were driving down the road. I was mad about something – I can't even remember what it was now.

"Have a nice day!" I said sarcastically. "I'm bummed out. *I'm* not having a nice day."

"Mom, every day is a nice day for me because I'm alive and I get to be with you."

How's that for putting me in my place when he was just a little boy? I felt so ashamed of myself. I am supposed to be the teacher, and he's teaching me how to behave. People should pay more attention to their children, especially when they're innocent before they go to school, the first six years of their life. Children are so incredibly brilliant and insightful.

Tim would always ask me such amazing questions. We were looking up at the brilliant blue sky one summer day and he asked me, "Mom, if there's a Heaven up above that sky, then there has to be a sky over that Heaven, right?"

"Yes, I suppose so." Truthfully, I don't think I'd given it a thought.

"In that case, then Heaven goes on and on, doesn't it? There's a Heaven above that one and a Heaven above that one and one above that one, and on and on."

I thought, "Well, why not? Who can say? Who *is* to say? And who are *we* to limit God?" We truly do need to have the faith of a little child.

If our will to do something good and our will to live is strong enough, no matter what obstacles we are faced with, we can do it. Just like the man who had no legs and only one arm was moving better and faster than the rest of us. If he can manage to do that, we should be ashamed of ourselves for sitting around acting like, "Well, I can't do this, I can't do that...."

Yes, we can do it.

*"You must learn to be still in the midst of activity
and to be vibrantly alive in repose."*

– Indira Gandhi

Prayer Time Is All The Time

We shouldn't pray only when we're in need of something. We must pray all the time.

Can we ever get enough practice at praying? No, so I say keep praying. The Scriptures tell us we're to pray all the time, about every issue. We can't always be down on our knees, of course, but we can pray in our hearts. We must be totally sincere and truthful. We must be reverent and humble.

I pray in the car at a stoplight or while driving down the highway. I guess if I'm ever stopped for speeding, I can say, "But officer, I was praying. I'm sorry, sir, I was caught up in the moment." That probably won't work, but I haven't tried it. I'd probably be ticketed for praying while driving through a "No-Pray Zone."

Anyway, I pray all the time in my heart and mind. It's important for me to get down on my knees and pray aloud in private. I'm not one of those people who gets up and prays in front of a bunch of people. I pray in a private way. I pray every day, and many times, out loud when I want to hear what I'm saying. The meditation I do every day is silent prayer and a time of rest for my body and my mind.

Prayers give thanks for all the good things surrounding us. Prayer focuses our attention on the good. It brings into focus all our blessings. We stop creating our own hell by looking for the good. Prayer does that for us; it shows us the good. And good is everywhere.

Look at the good we have around us. While walking through one of my favorite Nashville parks, in the summer, I move slowly because of the muggy heat, but I don't complain because it's hot. I'm glad I feel the heat and the humidity and can walk on my own two feet. Likewise, I don't complain when it's cold in the winter or rainy in the spring.

Many complain when it's hot and muggy in the summer and when it's cold and the trees don't have any leaves in the winter. What is their mindset? Are they unaware of the blessings they have? We must be grateful for the things we get free in this world. Walking in the park and enjoying the fresh air and the beautiful scenery, no matter what the season, it's all free, every bit of it. No charge. To be living where we're free to walk, talk, and say whatever is on our mind about anything or anybody…what kind of a miracle is that!

Many people ignore the bounties they're given, the everyday miracles. When you wake in the morning, it's a miracle to be aware of your life. If you can get up and go to the bathroom without assistance, it's another miracle. We must acknowledge, appreciate and be thankful for all our miracles all the time.

A cousin of mine is on dialysis and has been for many years while waiting for a kidney. Her life is one miracle after another. Every morning when I get up and go to the bathroom, I thank God I can urinate on my own. Through her affliction and suffering, I've observed how bravely she deals with it. She's an example to our entire family every minute of every day.

We should not overanalyze whether there is a spirit world or not, and how we got here and where we're going. We should be grateful that we *are* here and not worry about where we're going. We all have faults, but we should be as good as we can be whether or not we believe there is a hereafter. It's a choice we make. Every hour of every day, we are confronted with the opportunity to choose good or bad. I choose to be a blessing regardless of what happens. First of all, it is better for me personally because I feel good knowing I have made someone else feel better. Secondly, I feel good knowing that I was chosen to be an instrument of positive change instead of negative interaction with another.

I notice many people seem to be in the habit of negotiating with God for something they want. Who are we to bargain with God? Who do we think we are, "Well, now that you gave me life, God, I'll be good if I can go to Heaven." Isn't that a little bit one-sided?

God gave us everything. Through prayer, praise and worship, we begin to realize our potential. Matthew 18:19-20: *"Again I say unto you, that if two of you shall agree on earth as touching anything that they shall ask, it shall be done for them of my Father which is in Heaven. For where two or three are gathered together in my name, there I am in the midst of them."* Yes, God is good.

"It doesn't matter if it takes a long time getting there; the point is to have a destination."
– *Eudora Welty*

Let Fear Be Your Friend

Fear is one of the greatest emotions we can have. *"He said to his disciples, 'Why are you so afraid? Do you still have no faith?'" – Mark 4:40.*

Embracing our fear is necessary for survival. Whether it's fear of being injured or killed by a wild animal or the terror that moves us out of the way of a speeding train, fear is one of our best allies. It helps us become successful so that we don't become a ward of the state and a burden on society. If we fear being lost, we'll find a compass. Fear of failure certainly motivates you to succeed. Make sure that you make fear work *for* you and not *against* you.

Fear has been my constant companion, but it's pushed me onward. This is where faith comes in and how we can turn fear into faith just like flipping a coin. I choose to use fear as a positive emotion. We need only to quiet our minds long enough and not worry about what society thinks. We all possess an internal righting mechanism if we let our egos rest awhile.

We're more water than anything else, and every creature's life is like the rhythm of the ocean. Everyone has good and bad times – high tides and low tides in life. The ups and downs come and go like the seasons. Everything operates on rhythm. Life is all about rhythm. If we realize and understand that we control nothing but our attitude, then we can understand ourselves, enjoy ourselves and embrace ourselves – ultimately embrace life, by doing so we transfer this attitude to those around us. In musical terms, it's called getting in the groove.

It's all about choice and how much balance we want in our lives. Do we stay unbalanced because we are so obsessed with having something we don't need or something that's not good for us? It's our choice.

I have a girlfriend who has a lot on her plate. She was an only child. She's a gorgeous woman who married two financially successful men but neither relationship worked out. She had a daughter, with whom she never got along. They fought all the time.

Although the daughter had two small children, she had gotten into drugs. One night after partying, she staggered to her car and drove herself under a tractor-trailer. She lived but became a paraplegic.

Unfortunately, my friend suddenly found herself the sole caretaker of two grandchildren and her aging mother. She resented her daughter's rebellious ways. It was as if she was fighting herself all the time through fighting with her child.

Now that's a lot of stuff on one's plate. To realize your only child resents you, has two children, can't do a thing for herself or them and is costing you thousands of dollars a month for medical care and maintenance. You're suddenly faced with the situation of having these two grandchildren to raise. And your aging mother needs attention, and you're trying to run a business to boot. How does she handle all that?

I thought to myself, how would I handle her situation if faced with it? How would I get up every morning and go to work with all of this on my plate? Just the mental anguish and heartbreak of seeing my child in such a terrible shape and knowing that I'm in my mid-fifties with a demanding job, facing such an overwhelming responsibility.

I asked her about it and she answered with some words of wisdom. "Stella, there is just one way. You play the hand you're dealt. It's all I can do. I'm just playing my cards."

My friend evolved through all of this adversity. She taught me a great lesson. We all must play the hand we're dealt, but I say, don't just play the hand you're dealt. Seek the truth. Get in touch with yourself. Discover who *you* are and what you are made of, isn't that what life is about after all. You don't need to tell anyone else. You need only to tell yourself. Make the best of the hand you are holding, no matter what it is. Thank God, you have a hand at all and you have a chance to find a way to enrich your life.

That's what my girlfriend did. She had much to fear, but she made fear her ally by discovering her own courage. It led to the focus and determination she needed to make it through her darkest days.

Much has changed in her life. The boys are older now and able to care for themselves. Her daughter has done well with rehabilitation. And my friend has learned so much about herself through her aging mother. There's hope! She even found a wonderful husband during all of this. Time and patience has brought about these positive changes.

It's about love. It's *all* about love. That's the miracle here.

You will find your courage when you find your own truth. Not someone else's truth, but your own truth. Then you can fearlessly play the hand you're dealt.

If you're looking at darkness and dead ends, don't be afraid to seek help and advice. Get help when you need it from a counselor, minister, support group, friend or family member. We all have problems throughout our lives and help is there if we reach out.

Several years ago, I struggled with some major issues; I started attending Al-anon meetings, a support group for family members of alcoholics. I discovered that I was not the only person suffering, and my family wasn't the only one with alcoholics and drug addicts in it. I always felt alcohol and drug abuse was a choice made by the ones abusing. I was angry with some of my relatives for their choices. At Al-anon, I discovered positive ways to deal with these emotions, and it led me to some good books on the subject.

I recommend a book my son gave me: <u>Addiction Is A Choice</u>, by Jeffrey A. Schaler, Ph.D. It has many good points in it. An uncle recovering from alcohol addiction gave me the same advice that I found in Dr. Schaler's book, which is, we should be careful of the choices we make. As Maya Angelou says, "We *do* better when we *know* better." Let's all learn better ways to treat the ones we love, and ourselves.

Let's choose our addictions carefully. I've never known anyone to improve his or her life or the life of anyone else with drug and alcohol abuse, except maybe the liquor store or the bartender. Statistics say most domestic violence is because of alcohol abuse.

It's the same with gambling. Common sense tells me that if there were that many winners, those casinos wouldn't be so plush, and Las Vegas would be a ghost town. The only winners are the ones who own the places. Think about it – they are not in business to give all their money away.

I have two close friends who are seriously addicted to gambling. One has wasted her life savings and is afraid her husband will leave her when he finds out that she has gambled away all of their money. One day she told me on the phone that she was mad at God for not letting her win.

"God didn't tell you to gamble. You've left God out of it. You ought to pray before you go gambling the next time. Maybe you'll come to your senses and have the strength to stay out of those casinos."

Once again, we need to take responsibility for the choices we make and not be afraid to make the right choice.

*"To gain that which is worth having, it may
be necessary to lose everything."*
– Bernadette Devlin

My Latest Miracle

I don't have to look very far to find the most recent miracle in my life.

Every day when I walk out into the sunshine, see it, and feel it warming my skin, my little string of miracles begins.

Some days the sky is so blue and painted with massive cumulus clouds; and the air is clean and crisp and I breathe deep, filling my lungs with good feelings. I may walk with a friend. I may be enjoying my cat, a good book, or a good meal with family.

I'm not worrying at this point in my life.

I woke up without pain this morning. That's a miracle. Being born in America – that's another miracle for you. God truly blesses me and I'm passing it on.

The latest miracle is today. Tomorrow when the sun rises, I will start all over again being thankful.

I live for the next miracle with every breath I breathe, every blue sky, every dramatic cloud formation, every refreshing storm that cleanses the earth, every sunset, every sunrise, every wind chime, the sprinkle of laughter from a children's playground or the voice of my son saying, "Mom, I love you."

*"Once we give up searching for approval, we often
find it easier to earn respect and approval."*

– Gloria Steinem

Conclusion

Reading the things written here, I realize that I have so much yet to learn. I am neither a theologian nor an intellectual. I only know what my mind and heart tell me.

I believe that courage is our greatest weapon in life's battles. I believe that love does indeed conquer.

One morning I watched a morning talk show and a well-known politician spoke about the advisory committee to police the priests in the Catholic Church. He said the Catholic Church was "Christ's home on earth." Maybe so or maybe not. Where are the women or mothers on this committee? None were mentioned. I believe that God looks inside our hearts. We are not chosen according to gender, culture, or race.

Until we stop lying to ourselves and muster the courage to speak the truth about our own lives, things will not get better. The government and the church, as well as all big corporations are not immune to God's wrath. Although we live in the greatest country on the planet, we should not and cannot afford to believe things are okay.

Drugs and alcohol abuse destroy our families. Those of us who grew up without visible scars are still damaged for life. Little boys who see their fathers' abuse their mothers don't know anything else. Therefore, they repeat the same behavior in their own homes. Little girls who see this behavior don't know anything else, so they choose mates who treat them as their mothers were treated.

The police, the courts, and the community must be accountable. All must take a more aggressive role in preventing this behavior. Those who live in these situations need to know that they are not alone. There is help. If you are in an abusive situation, go to the phone and call the shelter, the police or tell your doctor, a friend or just someone. No one can help you if you don't help yourself by taking the first step.

I was disgusted by the way everyone treated Bill Clinton over his indiscretion. Yes, it was wrong. Let he who is without sin cast the first stone. Why did such a deed cause such a feeding frenzy in the media and among the politicians? Why did none of the politicians pray for him or with him? They just stood around and watched the crucifixion. None of them offered to pray for him. I prayed for him, I prayed for his daughter and his wife, and family. I also prayed for Monica.

My favorite people are the old and the young. The old, because they have wisdom - the young because they don't know there is a race to win.

Having faith in God supplies comfort in times of need. Follow your heart, use common sense and above all be kind to those less fortunate. Forgive yourself and then you can forgive others. The one simple truth remains - the core of all religions is love. Read again *I Corinthians 13:13 - "And now abideth faith, hope, charity, these three; but the greatest of these is charity."*

Love and respect your children, family and friends. When it's all said and done, you must run your own race, so make a good effort. Treat others with the same respect that you desire for yourselves; it's the Golden Rule.

I have been told often – as a criticism I might add – that I am "too honest." What does that mean? Sometimes, I make those close to me a bit uncomfortable. I assure you, that is not my intention. I'm just being myself. I may be too opinionated, too stubborn, too sensitive, but as Daddy would say, I have a tender heart. I hold no grudges. I have all I can handle trying to improve my own behavior.

A good friend says this about me, "Stella, you're just different, and you always say what everyone else is thinking. Most people won't say what they're thinking." My honesty does not come from me alone, but from God's spirit within me.

I continue to reclaim my joy by recognizing just how much God has blessed my family and me, being grateful for what I have now and remembering all the experiences I have had in the past.

I give thanks for my life. I see it as the precious miracle that it is.

Yes, there is much suffering in this world. Keeping a sense of humor while watching the six o'clock news is nearly impossible. There is so much gloom and doom going on around us. But much of it occurs through the actions of people and not from a wrathful God. Wouldn't it be great if all people could commit themselves to doing nothing but good in thought and action for just twenty-four hours? What change that would bring! We all want to go to heaven because by definition, it is a perfect place. The way we behave however, I don't know if God really is excited to have us show up and make a big mess of things like we have down here.

Truly though, we must believe in our families, our country, and ourselves and trust that God will never leave us. I know it sounds simple, but the truth is plain. What choice do we have anyway? Hold to your beliefs because that's all you have in this ever-changing world.

I'm sure I've opened my mouth and removed all doubt about the extent of my ignorance in this little book. So be it. The fact remains that I'm thankful to tell my story. I too, have a dream. I dream of a better home for women and children living in abusive situations. I dream that one day all my relatives will be kind to each other - respectful and considerate of each individual for their own uniqueness. I dream of husbands and wives getting along and taking care of one another. I dream there is enough to eat and a warm place to sleep for the poor and the hungry. I dream of all governments working together, helping each other and stopping the wars. I pray for an end to all sickness, disease and poverty. With God, all things are possible.

Our choices affect our lives. Let's be careful of the choices we make.

We must get rid of our differences. In God's eyes, we have no color, but the color of love. We have no gender. I believe we truly are all God's babies. It's in the scripture but religious people have twisted everything around to suit their own selfish agendas.

Destruction is sin. God is a creator not a destroyer. I thank God for His son and salvation. As I have done, I encourage you to get back in the "Word" and ask God for help and forgiveness and seek for more wisdom.

The more the change, the sweeter the memory
I wonder if you've changed half as much as me

I know I'd be better off if I could stop wondering
The more the change, the sweeter the memory

"The More The Change"
Written by: Stella Parton
©1977 My Mama's Music (BMI)

Most recently, I have had the opportunity to work in a number of independent films. I have also had my music on a number of film soundtracks as well. I continue to record and tour with a band of musicians. I have also been asked to speak at a number of events. Can you believe it? Me, a "motivational speaker?" I guess stranger things have happened. I certainly have always had an opinion. I think it's important to feed our minds positive thoughts. Otherwise, it's like junk food for the soul. How smart is that? I am thankful to have chosen to live a creative life. However, I have a problem with the "celebrity factor." It is a form of idolatry and the Bible speaks against it. I cannot believe how scandal is all you need to become an overnight sensation in this world. The churches and governments are full of hypocrisy. What a mess! As a friend of mine once said… "just think lovely thoughts, just think lovely thoughts." I continue to do that as much as possible.

I continue to find ways to help people in Appalachia. I've recorded a collection of coal mining songs called <u>American Coal</u>. I stay busy speaking out on behalf of the coal miners and their families. Thousands of jobs are being lost or taken away to other countries. Yet we continue to consume coal at a higher rate than ever before. I, too, would like to see more alternative energies, but in the meantime, don't rob the people in Appalachia. Where is the logic in that? So brace yourselves 'cause you'll be hearing more from me.

Stella Parton Discography

CHART SINGLES

Ragged Angel
Try Him You'll Like Him
I Want To Hold You In My Dreams
It's Not Funny Anymore
Ode To Olivia
The Mood I'm In
You've Crossed My Mind
Neon Woman (duet
   with Carmol Taylor)
I'm Not That Good At Goodbye
The Danger Of A Stranger
Standard Lie Number One
Four Little Letters
Undercover Lovers
Stormy Weather
Steady As The Rain
Room At The Top Of The Stairs

I'll Miss You
Young Love
Cross My Heart
I Don't Miss You Like I
   Used To
Legs
Picture In A Frame
Up In The Holler
I Draw From The Well
Smooth Talker
Keep On The Firing Line
Amazing Grace
This Little Light Of Mine
   Medley
Virtuous Woman
Family Ties
Tell It Sister Tell It

ALBUMS

In The Garden
Stella And The Gospel Carrolls
I Want To Hold You In My Dreams
Country Sweet
Stella Parton
Love Ya
The Best Of Stella Parton
So Far, So Good
True To Me
Always Tomorrow
Favorites, Vol. 1
Picture In A Frame
A Woman's Touch

Anthology
Appalachian Blues
Blue Heart
Appalachian Gospel
Favorites, Vol. 2
Favorites, Vol. 3
Songwriter Sessions
Holiday Magic
Testimony
Hits Collection
Mountain Rose
American Coal

BOOKS

Really Cookin', Vol. 1

Country Cookin'

VIDEOS

Cross My Heart (Music Video)

A Woman's Touch (Concert Video)

Up In The Holler (Music Video)

Appalachian Gospel
(Concert Video)
Live In Nashville
(Concert Video)

Domestic Violence Is A Crime!

Domestic violence is a major crime in our country. If you or anyone you know is in an abusive situation, you can get help by calling
1-800-799-SAFE

DOMESTIC VIOLENCE FACT SHEET

In the United States:

- Approximately 97% of the victims of domestic violence are women. (U.S. Department of Justice)

- A woman is battered every twelve seconds; over 3 million women are battered each year. (F.B.I.)

- Domestic violence is the single largest cause of injury to women, surpassing mugging, rapes, and car accidents combined. (Flitcraft and Stark)

- Each year, more than one million women seek medical assistance for injuries caused by battering. (Flitcraft and Stark)

- Approximately four women are murdered every day by their husband or boyfriend. (For Shelter and Beyond)

- Last year, domestic violence cost businesses an estimated four billion dollars in lost wages, benefits, and productivity. (MA Coalition of Battered Women Service Groups)

- One out of every two women will be involved in a violent relationship in their lifetime. This does not mean that one out of two men are abusive; only that batterers tend to go through many relationships without intervention to stop the violence. (Harvard Law School Battered Women's Advocacy Project)

- One out of eight Hollywood movies depicts a rape theme. By age 18, the average youth has watched 250,000 acts of violence and 40,000 attempted murders on TV. (Ms. Magazine)

- There are three times as many shelters for animals (3600) as there are for battered women and their children (1200). (Mintz Levin Project)

- At least 21% of all women who use emergency medical services are battered which means that 1.5 million women seek emergency medical treatment each year due to domestic violence. (National Institute of Mental Health)

The companion CD for "Tell It Sister Tell It"
is available on the internet at:

www.stellaparton.com

or write to:

**Attic Entertainment
P.O. Box 120871
Nashville, TN 37212
615-480-7054
615-331-4742 (fax)
atticent@gmail.com**

14176703R00128

Made in the USA
Charleston, SC
25 August 2012